D1612405

The German 88

The German 88

The Most Famous Gun of the Second World War

Terry Gander

Pen & Sword
MILITARY

First published in Great Britain in 2009 by
Pen & Sword Military
an imprint of
Pen & Sword Books Ltd
47 Church Street
Barnsley
South Yorkshire
S70 2AS

Copyright © Terry Gander, 2009

ISBN 978 1 84884 040 9

Printed and bound in the UK
by MPG Books

Pen & Sword Books Ltd incorporates the imprints of
Pen & Sword Aviation, Pen & Sword Family History, Pen & Sword Maritime,
Pen & Sword Military, Wharncliffe Local History, Pen & Sword Select,
Pen & Sword Military Classics, Leo Cooper, Remember When,
Seaforth Publishing and Frontline Publishing.

For a complete list of Pen & Sword titles please contact
PEN & SWORD BOOKS LIMITED
47 Church Street, Barnsley, South Yorkshire, S70 2AS, England
E-mail: enquiries@pen-and-sword.co.uk
Website: www.pen-and-sword.co.uk

Contents

Chapter 1

The Legend

By late 1941 word had spread throughout the Allied ranks that the Germans had a secret weapon that could knock out any Allied tank at ranges beyond which the recipients could not respond. This 'wonder weapon' exceeded all other anti-tank guns then in service in range, armour penetration capability and all-round firepower, and a military legend was born.

The weapon in question, the 8.8cm FlaK 18 or 36, went on to become the most widely known of all German artillery pieces and was so feared that even now it retains the title of the most famous gun of the Second World War, despite the long list of other potential candidates for that title. In 1941 Allied intelligence personnel sought desperately to learn the 'secrets' of what became generally known to them as the '88'. It emerged that the 88 had not been designed primarily as an anti-tank weapon but was in fact an anti-aircraft gun (*FlugzeugabwehrKanone* or *FliegerabwehrKanone* – hence FlaK) pressed into the anti-armour role to utilise its latent firepower against ground targets, among which were the unfortunate Allied tanks.

In time the 88s grew into a family that encompassed dedicated tank and anti-tank guns as well as anti-aircraft guns, while numerous sub-variants, including self-propelled platforms, were to appear as the war continued. With time, more technically advanced models of the 88 were to materialise to expand the 88 family into three distinct branches, each with its own specific type of 88mm ammunition, and the group grew further still when captured Soviet anti-aircraft guns were converted to fire German 88mm ammunition. The 88, in its original anti-aircraft form, was one of the few German weapons that remained in series production throughout the war years. It became one of the mainstays of the German air-defence forces, for both the *Heer* (Army) and *Luftwaffe* (Air Force), and its deployment spread to other non-German armed forces as well. For some of these non-German armed forces the 88 remained a viable weapon until almost the end of the twentieth century.

The 88 did not spring out of nowhere. Had they but taken more notice of the fact, the 88 had been an anti-armour option within the German tactical establishment since the Spanish Civil War of 1936–1939. The unfortunate

The starting point, the 8.8cm FlaK 18. (TJ Gander Collection)

British Expeditionary Force (BEF) had first experienced the 88 in combat at Arras in May 1940; and the French had suffered from its firepower during the earlier Meuse crossings. By mid-1941 the 88 was making its lethal presence felt on the battlefields of North Africa and by the end of that year it was adding to its laurels on the post-Operation Barbarossa Eastern Front. From 1939 onwards the 88 acted as the mainstay of the air defence of the *Dritter Reich*.

The origins of the 88 can now be traced back to 1916, if not before.

Beginnings

By 1916 military aircraft were beginning to make a significant impact on the tactical situation prevailing on the battlefields of the First World War, especially on the Western Front. Although aviation was still in its infancy in 1916, increasing use was being made of aircraft for reconnaissance and artillery observation, while the first tentative experiments in tactical bombing were being conducted. On both sides, by 1916 air-to-air combat was well established in attempts to deny the enemy the advantages of observing their actions or dispositions. Ground forces also sought some form of weapon with which to counter the airborne threat, not only against aircraft but also against observation balloons.

As far as the Germans were concerned the military balloon had been a potential adversary ever since the Franco-Prussian War of 1870. Various high

Early days.
The Erhardt/Rheinmetall 5cm
Ballon Abwehr Kanone *(BAK)*
of 1906. (TJ Gander Collection)

barrel-elevation gun projects were mooted during the years that followed and in 1906 the German Erhardt concern (later to become part of the Rheinmetall-Borsig conglomerate) mounted a 5cm *Ballon Abwehr Kanone* (BAK) on an armoured truck chassis and demonstrated it to an unimpressed German General Staff. Daimler followed in 1909 with a 5.7cm FlaK *Panzerkraftwagen*. Neither of these vehicles was accepted for service, although the concept was to re-emerge before the end of 1914.

A 1908 experiment combining a 6.5cm Rheinmetall gun with an Erhardt truck chassis. The vehicle and gun had a crew of six and, powered by a 80hp engine, could reach road speeds of up to 60km/h, while the gun itself could fire up to 25rds/min and reach an maximum altitude of 7,900m. This gun and vehicle combination remained a prototype. (TJ Gander Collection)

As early as 1914 a small German anti-aircraft arm had been formed. When the First World War began this infant arm was equipped with just eighteen guns. Most of them were simply field guns, usually of 77mm calibre, with their field carriages perched on precarious frameworks to provide the necessary high angles of barrel elevation and some degree of on-carriage traverse to track potential targets. As the usual barrel length was limited to about 27 calibres, the modest muzzle velocities resulted in extended times of projectile flight to the target and range was limited. Something better was needed and requests for more powerful, custom-built anti-aircraft weapons were placed with German industry. The result was a series of 57, 75, 77 and 80mm high-velocity guns with extended length barrels (to enhance muzzle velocities) and more serviceable high-elevation mountings. Some were positioned on self-propelled mountings. During late 1916 the first 88mm guns appeared.

The selection of the 88mm calibre was as a result of the fact that 88mm guns had long been established as standard German Navy weapons, mainly because a round of 88mm ammunition was the considered to be the largest and heaviest that a single man could handle as a fixed round, i.e. the projectile and propellant-carrying cartridge case were joined together as a single unit for loading to increase the possible rate of fire (the total round weight was 15.3kg). Production machinery for both barrels and ammunition was therefore readily to hand at the production facilities of Krupp AG and Rheinmetall-Borsig AG (hereafter referred to simply as Rheinmetall), and both produced the requested *Geschütze 8.8cm KwFlaK* (*Kw – Kampfwagen* – military vehicle).

The Krupp and Rheinmetall submissions emerged as almost identical designs. Both had 45-calibre barrels (i.e. the barrel length was 45 times the calibre of 88mm) that could fire a 9.6kg high-explosive, time-fuzed projectile (also of naval

An example of a Rheinmetall Geschütze 8.8cm KwFlaK *ready for action with its L/45 barrel at maximum elevation.*
(P Chamberlain Collection)

A surviving example of the Krupp version of the Geschütze 8.8cm KwFlaK *still on display at the Aberdeen Proving Ground Museum in Maryland.* (TJ Gander)

origin) at a muzzle velocity of from 765 to 785m/s to a practical operational height of about 6,850m. Maximum possible range was 10,800m. Both near-identical mountings were secured on flat-platform, twin-axled trailers that were stabilised in action by folding outrigger arms on each side. One advanced feature was that the trailer mountings were intended from the outset to be towed by motorised tractors, a most unusual procedure in 1916 and one that gave the guns a high degree of mobility. Their total towed weight was approximately 7,300kg. Aiming was primarily by on-carriage, direct-vision methods, but by late 1918 rudimentary forms of centralised fire control were being introduced.

Head-on view of the Krupp version of the Geschütze 8.8cm KwFlaK *at the Aberdeen Proving Ground Museum in Maryland.* (TJ Gander)

By the end of 1918 the German anti-aircraft arm was no more. What anti-aircraft guns had survived the events leading up to the November 1918 Armistice were impounded by the Allies, either to be scrapped or handed out as war trophies, few of which seem to have survived. As the newly formed *Reichswehr* was intended to be limited in scope to the functions of an internal security force, the integral air defence for the German land forces was almost entirely dependent on rifle-calibre machine-guns, other than a few batteries (code-named *Fahrabteilung*) of Rheinmetall 75mm guns with 60-calibre barrels, which were considered to be unsatisfactory and destined to be sold to Spain as soon as 88s began to arrive. But already plans for the next steps in the 88 story were being made.

Development

The terms of the 1919 Treaty of Versailles imposed stringent sanctions on the German armament industrial infrastructure, and especially on the twin industrial giants of Krupp and Rheinmetall. Krupp AG of Essen was particularly affected, for it was forbidden by specific clauses in the Treaty from designing and manufacturing artillery having calibres below 170mm, a market sector that it had virtually made its own and from which it had hitherto gained the bulk of its income. In addition, the number of guns it could manufacture each year was strictly limited. As a result, during the early 1920s Krupp (and Rheinmetall) activities were constantly monitored by teams of Treaty observers to ensure the Treaty terms were being obeyed and implemented, so senior executives sought some way to overcome the restrictions that hampered their on-going commercial ambitions.

The strategy followed by Rheinmetall, as well as Krupp, was to form associations with defence manufacturers outside Germany and therefore not under the unwelcome gaze of the Treaty observers. Rheinmetall went on to develop links with concerns in Holland and Switzerland, while Krupp renewed a close association with AB Bofors of Sweden – the two concerns had previously created various forms of co-operation and licensing relationships dating from the 1880s (the first gun manufactured by AB Bofors was built under licence from Krupp).

The new Bofors/Krupp association was established by 1921. In broad terms a team of Krupp designers (at first just three) and technicians were allowed to utilise the AB Bofors facilities at Karlskoga in Sweden in return for access to Krupp manufacturing licences and techniques, design expertise and general know-how. AB Bofors provided access to their research and design premises and activities. Krupp also purchased an interest in the AB Bofors concern. As the 1920s progressed Bofors and Krupp personnel co-operated on a range of new artillery designs, and artillery and ballistic research in general. By 1922 the German part of this relationship was being surreptitiously subsidised by the German War Office. Together with Krupp AG the War Office established a 'ghost' office in Berlin named Koch und Kienzle, through which funds could be channelled to finance the team in Sweden without attracting scrutiny from Treaty observers or the German parliament.

Many of the co-operative Bofors/Krupp projects undertaken during the 1920s remained as 'paper' designs. However, one destined to reach the hardware stage was a 75mm anti-aircraft gun with a 60-calibre barrel which was intended to be able to cope with aerial targets having performances well above those of contemporary aircraft. The intention was that such a gun would meet a stated Swedish armed forces requirement and perhaps form the basis for the next generation of German anti-aircraft guns. An 80mm version was proposed to meet possible export orders, while 76.2mm variants were manufactured and delivered to the Soviet Union and Finland. Under the Bofors label, 75mm guns were ordered by the Swedish armed forces in both static and mobile forms and others were exported to nations such as Brazil. More 75mm guns were sent to Germany, but only in small numbers. They were adopted by the German Navy, most of them ending up defending German dockyard facilities.

But the German Army was less impressed. By the late 1920s the terms of the Treaty of Versailles were gradually becoming moribund and staff planners were increasingly taking measures to determine the nature of the next generation of weapons they considered necessary for the future. Using data gleaned from the operational reports of 1914–1918 they had decided that of the two artillery

One of the results of the Krupp/Bofors association was the 76.2mm Model 1927 sold to Finland. This example now serves as a war memorial on the island fortress of Suomenlinna (Sveaborg) off Helsinki. (TJ Gander)

calibres allowed to them by the Treaty terms to arm the *Reichswehr*, namely 75mm and 105mm, neither was suitable for the field-service, 'heavy' anti-aircraft gun that they forecast would be needed. The 75mm calibre was regarded as too light in projectile terms, while a 105mm fixed round was considered to be too bulky and heavy to be handled comfortably by an individual. Once again, the 88mm calibre formed a convenient intermediary. The experience gained with their Bofors counterparts indicated to Krupp designers that the earlier Krupp/Bofors 75mm design could be readily utilised as the basis for an 88mm gun.

By 1930 the Krupp/Bofors association was in the process of winding down. In that year the Swedish government passed an edict that severely restricted the ownership of Swedish firms by overseas concerns. The Krupp teams therefore returned to Essen, taking with them the drawings of what was to become the basis for the 88. Once back in Essen, refinements were added and suitable enlargements of the Bofors/Krupp design were introduced so that by the beginning of 1932 the prototypes of the 88mm gun were ready for testing.

Soon after the initial testing phase the first production plans were quietly made so that when Hitler's *Nationalsozialistische Deutsche Arbeiterpartie* (NSDAP) came to power in 1933, the last vestiges of any acknowledgement of the existence of the Treaty of Versailles could be cast aside and series production could commence almost immediately. By the end of 1933 the first examples of the 88 were in the hands of the *Wehrmacht*, the newly formed all-services descendant of the old *Reichswehr*, although full series production on the desired scale did not commence until early 1936. The new gun was designated as the

An early photograph of a Luftwaffe gun crew preparing an 8.8cm FlaK 18 for firing.
(P Chamberlain Collection)

An 8.8cm FlaK 18 with the barrel at near maximum elevation. Note that the gun still has its loading tray in position — they were often removed as they were awkward to use. (P Chamberlain Collection)

A pre-war training exercise in the Ruhr being undertaken by the crew of an 8.8cm FlaK 18. (TJ Gander Collection)

8.8cm FlaK 18, the '18' being bestowed as an unconvincing measure to denote that the design dated back to 1918. That was one of the very last steps taken to mislead the increasingly redundant Treaty observers.

The crew of an 8.8cm FlaK 18 taking a rest to pose for the camera during a pre-1939 training exercise. Note that the prime mover for the gun is some form of heavy truck. (TJ Gander Collection)

Modifications

The 8.8cm FlaK 18 was an immediate success. Intended for employment against tactical bombers, it was a semi-automatic weapon in that when the gun fired the recoil was used to eject the spent cartridge case and re-cock the firing mechanism ready to fire once the next round was inserted into the breech, either by hand or with a power-assisted rammer. The highly mobile carriage platform had wheeled axle bogie 'halves' fore and aft (designed by the firm of Lindner), from which the cruciform firing platform was lowered for action. Once in action the maximum possible barrel traverse was two full 360° arcs in either direction, that is the barrel could traverse a full 360° plus a second 360° if necessary. There were two fold-up side arms, one each side, which could be lowered to add to the firing stability. The overall ballistic performance of the 56-calibre gun and its ammunition was more than adequate to tackle any aircraft then contemplated for future service. With a trained crew the gun could fire up to twenty rounds each minute, although a maximum of fifteen rounds per minute was more usual.

Good as the FlaK 18 was in 1933, the German *Heereswaffenampt* (HWA, roughly equivalent to the old British Ministry of Supply) foresaw the need for some modifications to the barrel and its manufacturing methods. These modifications were to make a sizeable impact on the 88 story so are worthy of further description, and give an indication of the detail in which the German

A factory fresh 8.8cm FlaK 18, probably photographed during testing at the Krupp proofing range at Hillersleben. (P Chamberlain Collection)

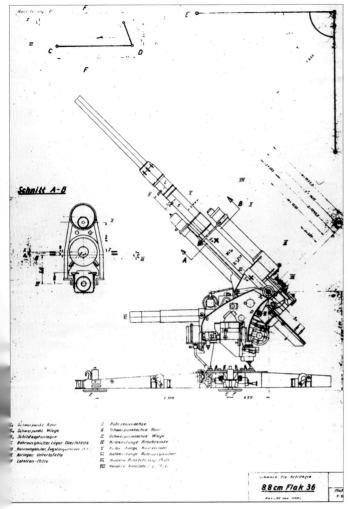

Despite its quality this drawing of an 8.8cm FlaK 36 is important as it was taken from an original factory negative and shows the main side-on features of the classic model of the 88 series. (TJ Gander Collection)

military establishment was prepared to indulge in their preparations for their foreseen future conflict.

The 8.8cm FlaK 18 had a conventional one-piece (monobloc) barrel. Using the cordite-type propellant and high-explosive projectiles with copper driving bands, both still in widespread use in 1933, this resulted in a service life of about 900 rounds before the barrels became too worn for further practical use. This service life was regarded as too short by the German war planners, who anticipated a European war of short duration but of great intensity, to the point where large numbers of worn FlaK 18 barrels would need to be replaced, probably under field conditions, imposing great strains on extended transport and repair facilities. In addition, creating stockpiles of complete replacement barrels would be prohibitively expensive and difficult because of the relative

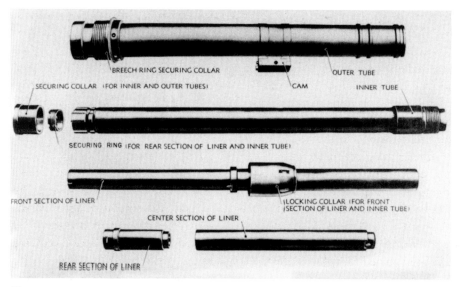

The main components of the Rohr Aufbau 9 *(RA 9 – barrel construction 9). This illustration was taken from the* TM E-9 369A manual *on the 8.8cm FlaK 36 prepared by the US Army in June 1943.* (US National Archives)

shortages of the necessary high-quality raw materials involved.

For the first time Rheinmetall of Düsseldorf played a part in the FlaK 18/36/37 story. The barrel-life problem was passed to this company (no doubt because Krupp was by then busy to the point of being overwhelmed) and it devised a solution that may have been elegant in engineering terms but one that was to have unfortunate results in the longer term. It designed a three-piece-barrel solution based around the fact that most barrel wear takes place at the forcing cone (where the neck of the cartridge case ends) and the first few calibres of rifling. With the Rheinmetall plan the modified barrel, known as the *Rohr Aufbau 9* (RA 9 – barrel construction 9), consisted of a jacket, a sleeve and an inner tube in three sections, the centre section of which carried the forcing cone and the first part of the rifling. A locking collar secured the breech assembly to the jacket and the three-part inner tube was held within the sleeve by a clamping collar towards the front of the barrel and a clamping ring at the rear. To change the inner sections the barrel could be stripped down to its component parts by field technicians, or even the gun crew, in order to replace just the worn centre section. As an added measure to reduce wear on the centre section a slight reduction in the initial projectile spin rate inside the barrel was introduced – the emergent spin rate remained as before.

There was therefore no longer any need to stockpile complete replacement barrels. Only the relatively small centre sections of the inner tube needed to be held ready for use somewhere near the guns. References to the RA 9 can be found as the *Ersatzrohre für 8.8cm FlaK 18, 36 und 37*. The original one-piece FlaK 18 barrel became the RA 1.

Needless to say, the RA 9 had its shortcomings. One was that high-priced (and scarce), high-quality steels had to be used in the construction as the separate components lacked the rigidity that would have been imparted by a conventional one-piece construction. Manufacture involved very close machining tolerances, especially relating to the inner sections, and the number of skilled man hours required during manufacture was well in excess of those needed for a more conventional barrel assembly. In addition, the weight of the finished product was greater than that for a conventional barrel so carriage components such as the recoil and equilibrator mechanisms had to be modified or adjusted accordingly.

At the time all these shortcomings were recognised and accepted as the RA 9 conferred all the advantages needed of it. However, once large-scale experience had been gained further modifications had to be introduced. The system had to be altered to a two-section inner barrel, a measure made necessary by the joint between the chamber and the forcing cone sections wearing too quickly. This unforeseen wear was introduced by gas leakage plus the ravages of the almost inevitable abrasive debris introduced on the fixed rounds as they were loaded. In addition, the same joint, covered by the front end of the cartridge case, proved to be prone to slight temperature-expansion differences that expanded the thin-walled cartridge case into the joint, leading to hard-case extractions and the resultant jams. The only immediate way to overcome these shortcomings was to manufacture the RA 9 chamber and centre inner barrel sections in one piece rather than two.

The introduction of the RA 9 to the gun and carriage during 1937 resulted in a new service designation, that of 8.8cm FlaK 36. This '36' model could be readily identified visually by the prominent clamping collar some two-thirds of the way along the barrel. The original FlaK 18 barrel had a smooth, tapering profile along its entire length.

In time the multi-section principles of the RA 9 were retained by Rheinmetall for the early production examples of the 8.8cm FlaK 41 (of which more later) and the 10.5cm FlaK 38 and 39, but as the war continued the advantages of the multi-section barrel faded away. One of the main reasons for this unforeseen situation was the introduction of new propellants such as Diglycol and Gudol, which burned at lower temperatures then the old propellants and thus caused much less barrel wear and erosion. Another factor was the replacement of copper driving bands by sintered iron bands developed by the Kaiser-Wilhelm-Gesellschaft of Düsseldorf, which named its new product as *Weichstahl*. Sintered iron (*Sintereisen*) also produced less wear, in addition to being less costly than

Two captured guns display the main recognition difference between the 8.8cm FlaK 18 and 36. The example in the foreground is a FlaK 18, while the FlaK 36 in the background clearly shows its distinctive barrel outline. (TJ Gander Collection)

scarce copper. These two factors combined to increase barrel life to at least 6,000 rounds and sometimes as much as 10,000 rounds, so the main reason for the multi-section barrels disappeared. Over-extended German industrial plants were left to mass-produce expensive multi-section barrels requiring costly high-quality steels and an excessive number of skilled man hours at a time when they could be least afforded. Production lines could not be easily reorganised for simpler methods without disrupting the flow of much-needed finished equipments to the field, so it was not until the last year of the war that it became possible to return to a simplified, divided monobloc barrel for the 88 anti-aircraft gun series. The choice of a divided monobloc construction was enforced rather than selected as nearly all the machine tools then available in the manufacturing plants had been designed to produce multi-section barrels and were therefore not large enough to be converted to fabricate one-piece barrels. By the end of the war in 1945, some 88mm monobloc barrels were beginning to be manufactured at the Skoda-Werke at Pilsen following the introduction of a novel vertical centrifuge casting process.

With the advantage of hindsight, it can now be said that the introduction of the RA 9 formed a typical example of German war planning that went badly wrong as the Second World War lasted much longer than German war planners had expected.

More modifications

As mentioned above, the conversion of the 8.8cm FlaK 18 to accommodate the heavier RA 9 barrel resulted in a new designation, that of 8.8cm FlaK 36. Also introduced on the new gun was a revised carriage system, the *Sonderanhänger 201*. Although there were other changes, the main alteration was to the revised carriage the complete gun and carriage was towed on, with the barrel pointing to the rear. This arrangement was introduced following early combat experience with the FlaK 18 in Spain, where the guns were deployed by German Condor Legion 'volunteers' serving on the Nationalist side during the Civil War. That experience involved not only air-defence employment but also the growing use of the 88 as an indirect-fire artillery piece that could outrange most contemporary field

A Luftwaffe *gunner posing on an 8.8cm* FlaK 36 *emplaced in a semi-permanent static installation.* (P Chamberlain Collection)

Detailed illustration of the left-hand side of an 8.8cm FlaK 36 *taken from the American* TM E-9 369A manual. (US National Archives)

REAR BOGIE   FRONT BOGIE

An illustration of the original version of the Sonderanhänger 201 *carrying an 8.8cm FlaK 36, also taken from the* TM E-9 369A manual. (US National Archives)

artillery, and eventually to the direct-fire anti-tank and ground-target role. In the latter instances it was soon discovered that the in and out of action times could be reduced if the barrel was kept pointing to the rear. However, provision was made so that the gun and carriage could still be towed with the barrel pointed in the direction of travel, if such an arrangement was thought necessary.

The combat experience gained in Spain was to prove of great importance to the 88 series during the Second World War. By 1939 another revised limber system had been introduced, this time the *Sonderanhänger 202*, the main visual change being the introduction of two road wheels on each wheel station, with the suspension revised accordingly. On earlier models only the rear bogie 'wheel half' had two road wheels, so the two 'wheel halves' were not inter-changeable. On the *Sonderanhänger 202* the extra wheels not only provided for a smoother ride over rough terrain but the gun could be more readily fired from off its road wheels whenever the tactical situation demanded such a course of action – firing from the lowered cruciform platform remained the preferred option. Once the twin-wheel arrangement had been installed the two-wheel bogies became inter-changeable. Other changes involved the carriage levelling gear.

The 'twin-wheel' *Sonderanhänger 202* proved to be so successful that, when possible, they were retrofitted to the FlaK 18 and early models of the FlaK 36, even if the total towed weight of the gun and carriage was increased from about 7,000kg to 8,200kg. The nominal cost to the *Reich* also increased. Whereas a FlaK 18 had an accounting cost of RM 31,750, that for a FlaK 36 was RM

An 8.8cm FlaK 36 on a Sonderanhänger 202 with the barrel pointing to the rear. (P Chamberlain Collection)

33,600. By 1940 gun shields (some with hinged sides) had been added to many guns, especially to those supporting ground formations – shields were not often provided for home or static defence guns.

One further variant was to be added to the 88 FlaK series, namely the 8.8cm FlaK 37 which, with its revised fire-control transmission system, entered service during late 1939. On the 8.8cm FlaK 18 and FlaK 36 fire control against aircraft targets was conducted using a centralised fire-command centre where an electro-mechanical predictor, the *Kommandogerät 36* or *40*, calculated rangefinder, tracking

The end of an 8.8cm FlaK 36 in North Africa with the gun, complete with shield, on a Sonderanhänger 202. (P Chamberlain Collection)

and other target data to determine where the target would be when a fired projectile had taken the time to reach the same position in space. To ensure the gun barrels were pointing in the correct and desired direction, a constant flow of laying data was transmitted to each gun via 108-core electrical cables. On the gun a system known as the *Ubertragungsgerät 30* (UTG 30) comprised a display of three concentric circles of small lamp bulbs which the layers had to follow mechanically by turning control wheels to move pointers of corresponding lengths to cover the bulbs as they lit up. One display array was used for barrel elevation and a second for traverse (azimuth). Control of covering the lamps and thus the barrel position was carried out using two hand wheels on the right-hand side of the carriage. The wheel towards the rear controlled barrel elevation, while that to the front controlled traverse. The laying gear could be disconnected mechanically to allow large traverse changes to be made more rapidly by one of the crew pulling or pushing the upper carriage around. On a few guns, believed to be limited to about fifty, the dials were arranged so that one operator could control both traverse and elevation, but it was more usual to involve two personnel for the anti-aircraft laying task.

The two fire-control data-display dials on a Finnish 8.8cm FlaK 37. (TJ Gander)

On the 8.8cm FlaK 37 this light-bulb and pointer arrangement was replaced by a simpler selsyn or 'follow the pointer' data display system known as the *Ubertragungsgerät 37* (UTG 37). In place of light bulbs the UTG 37 featured dials with motor-driven moving pointers which the layer had to follow, again mechanically, by turning a control wheel. The UTG 37 proved to be much easier, smoother and quicker to utilise than the UTG 30 and had the added advantage that it could be readily integrated into radar-controlled fire-control systems. In addition, the data-transmission cables involved required only forty-six cores and the overall system proved to be much easier to maintain than the earlier light-bulb and pointer arrangement.

It might be expected that the FlaK 37 would accommodate the multi-section RA 9 barrel assembly and many did, although in practice existing or refurbished FlaK 18 one-piece barrels were used.

The 8.8cm FlaK 37 was intended to be deployed only for the relatively static defence of the home *Reich*, although exceptions occurred. For instance, in 1945 the Royal Norwegian Air Force took over no less than 194 examples (55 mobile, 139 static) of the 8.8cm FlaK 37 that had been left behind by the *Luftwaffe* when the Germans left Norway. In addition, ninety FlaK 37 guns were sold to Finland during 1943 and 1944.

The Meuse Crossings

By 1939 the German General Staff had outlined plans for the invasion of most of their neighbouring nations, including the old enemy France. Most of these 'paper' strategies envisaged a conventional attack very much along First World One lines, for at that time the potential of the Panzer divisions was still not fully appreciated by many. However, it was accepted that any invading force moving against France would have to encounter the Maginot Line, the line of formidable fortifications that covered the entire length of France's border with Germany (and Italy).

Exactly how these extensive fortifications were to be overcome occupied a great deal of the General Staff's planning time. Schemes were devised for super-heavy artillery to blast a way through the French defences, but that was an expensive and time-consuming measure that would take time to develop. One alternative was actually to test similar fortifications to see if some other methods could be utilised. During 1938, the opportunity arose to do just that when the Czecho-Slovak Sudetenland defences passed intact into German hands following the infamous Munich Agreement.

French technicians had advised the Czechs regarding their defensive line in such a way as to make any German attack on Czecho-Slovakia a costly proposition, so the Czechs had therefore incorporated many advanced features that had been added to the Maginot Line fortifications. The Germans were therefore able to study the Czech forts in detail and determine exactly how they could be subdued, if not taken. By early 1939 reports from Spain included numerous mentions of how the Nationalist Spanish Army had utilised their 88s to defeat field fortifications. German artillery officers decided to take one step further and see how they would fare against full-scale fortifications, the Sudetenland defences being their experimental cockpit.

Their live-firing experiments included all manner of artillery pieces apart from the 88s, but it soon became apparent that the 88s were very effective against steel-weapon embrasures and observation cupolas and apertures set into concrete, thereby effectively disarming and blinding the fortifications. The experiment results added their emphasis to the development of armour-piercing rounds for the 88, the Maginot Line defences then being the prime target for such ammunition.

When the time came for the invasion of France in May 1940 the Maginot Line was no longer in the forefront of the General Staff's collective mind. The bold selection of Operation Sichelschnitt (literally Operation Sickle Cut), the invasion of France through the neutral Belgian Ardennes by concentrated tank formations, had been made. The intention was that the Maginot Line would be by-passed (the Line did not extend north into the Ardennes) so there would be no need to attack it. As always, there was a drawback to this plan but it was relatively insignificant compared to battering a way through the Maginot Line.

The drawback was the River Meuse, which made its way across the planned invasion route. The Meuse was well known to the German Army from their operations during the Franco-Prussian War of 1870 and in 1940 its significance as a defensive measure was well appreciated by the French. By 1940 virtually every potential crossing point had been covered by well-sited fortified structures, which varied from what the British termed pillboxes to extensive bunkers provided with anti-tank guns and machine-guns and supported by infantry. All existing bridges were prepared for demolition so the Germans

German troops dragging an 8.8cm FlaK 18 over a pontoon bridge thrown across the Meuse after the opposing French bunkers had been neutralised by 88 fire. (P Chamberlain Collection)

knew they would have to face that most hazardous of military operations, a river crossing against prepared defences.

The Meuse defences were to be tested on 13 May 1940, around and to the north of Sedan. Having made their way through the Ardennes, three Panzer Corps were to be involved in the crossing but with no fixed bridges available to them the initial stages of the crossings had to be carried out by combat engineers (*Pioniere*) using small assault boats.

In nearly all cases the initial crossings went badly. Conventional artillery was in most cases unable to neutralise the defending bunkers, while the soon to be infamous *Stuka* dive bombers were often too inaccurate or their bombs were unable to penetrate the concrete coverings of the structures. As a result casualties among the first wave of combat engineers were heavy and few crossings proved successful. A typical example was the crossing near the built-up suburb of Floing to the west of Sedan, where tanks and *Sturmgewehr* assault guns were lined up across the river from the bunkers to cover the initial stages of the operation. Their guns soon proved to be unable to knock out the defending bunkers on the far side of the river so the combat-engineer crossings failed in the face of well-directed machine-gun fire.

It was not until an 88 was manhandled through the streets approaching the river that the opposing French bunkers could be overcome. That single gun was able to fire directly against the French weapon embrasures and damage the defending weapons, wound or disable the bunker occupants with projectile splinters or destroy the bunkers altogether by punching holes through their structures. Only a few of the French bunkers had to be dealt with in this fashion for the occupants of the surviving ones, their morale already shaky, soon realised what was happening and made their escape while they still could. As a result more combat engineers were able to make their way across the river in relative safety and, once on the other side, they could start making their preparations for the construction of the pontoon and assault bridging that would enable the Panzers to cross the Meuse and commence their offensive moves towards the still distant Channel coast. Similar action sequences occurred at almost all the Meuse crossing points.

Without the direct fire of those 88s against the French bunkers, the Meuse crossings of 13 May 1940 would have been either severely delayed or costly in casualties. As it was, they did delay the German advance for a while, and German casualties were significant (but lighter than anticipated), but the deployment of a few 88s made the German operation a complete success.

The illustrations on the following pages show the 8.8cm FlaK 18 from a variety of angles. (All drawings from P Chamberlain Collection)

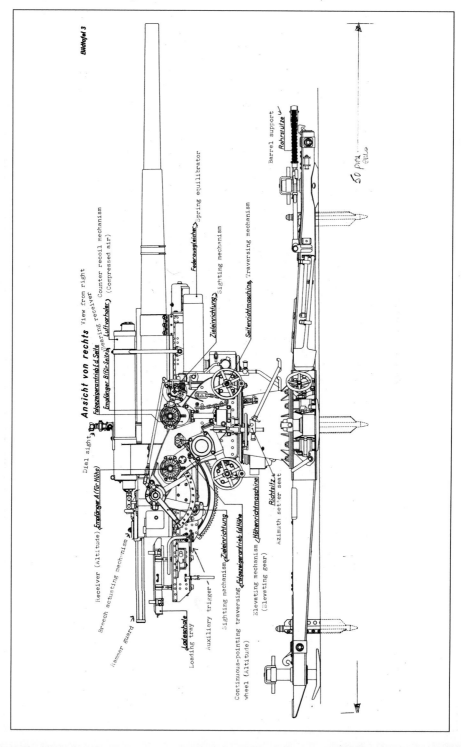

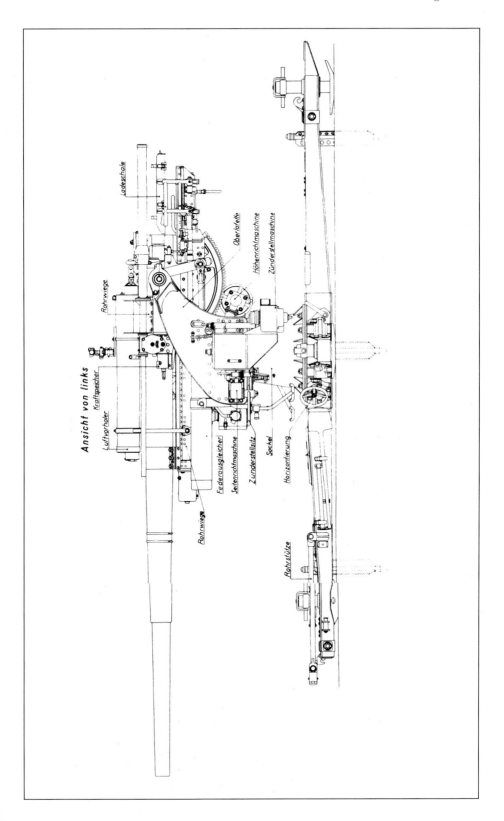

Ansicht von links

Ladeschale

Oberlafette

Höhenrichtmaschine

Zünderstellmaschine

Rohrwiege

Kraftspeicher

Luftvorholer

Rohrwiege

Federausgleicher

Seitenrichtmaschine

Zünderstellsitz

Sockel

Horizontierung

Rohrstütze

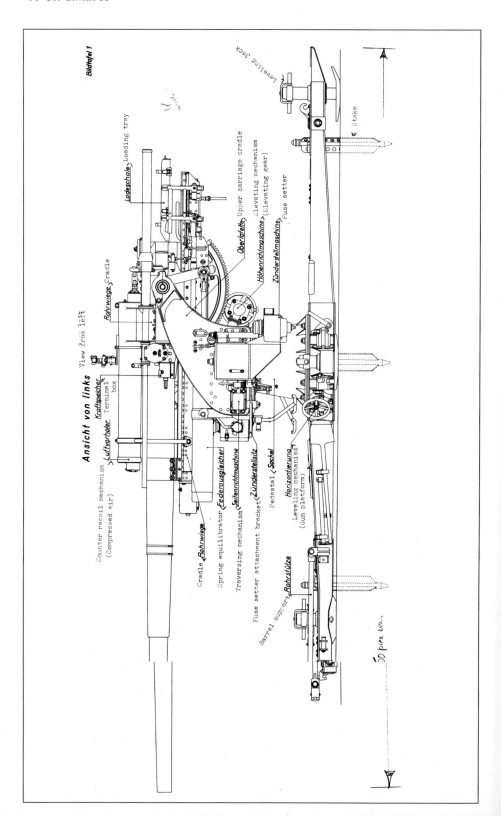

Bildtafel 1

Ansicht von links View from left

Counter recoil mechanism
(Compressed air)

Kraftspeicher
Luftvorholer Terminal box

Ladeschale Loading tray

Rohrwiege Cradle

Oberlafette Upper carriage cradle
Höhenrichtmaschine (Elevating mechanism) (Elevating gear)
Zünderstellmaschine Fuse setter

Leveling Jack

Stake

Cradle *Rohrwiege*
Spring equilibrator *Federausgleicher*
Traversing mechanism *Seitenrichtmaschine*
Fuse setter attachment bracket *Zünderstellsitz*
Pedestal *Sockel*
Horizontierung Leveling mechanism (Gun platform)

Barrel support *Rohrstütze*

50 p\u00e9ra ......

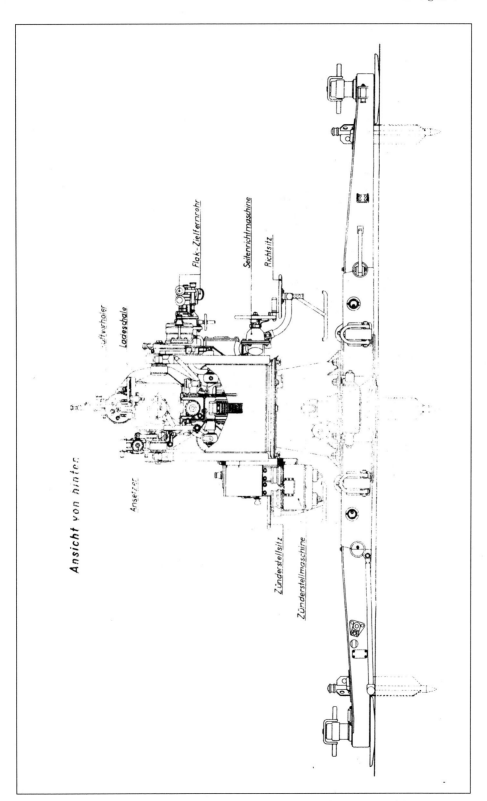

Ansicht von hinten.

Luftvorholer
Ladeschale
Flak-Zielfernrohr
Seitenrichtmaschine
Richtsitz
Ansetzer
Zünderstellsitz
Zünderstellmaschine

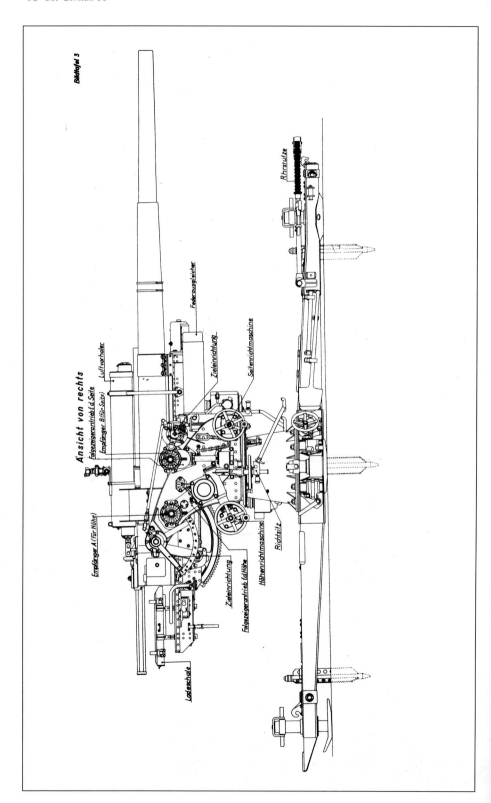

Bildtafel 3

Ansicht von rechts

Folgezeigerantrieb f.d. Seite
Empfänger B (für Seite)
Luftvorholer
Zieleinrichtung
Federausgleicher
Seitenrichtmaschine
Rohrstütze

Empfänger A (für Höhe)
Zieleinrichtung
Folgezeigerantrieb f.d.Höhe
Höhenrichtmaschine
Richtsitz

Ladeschale

Descriptions: FlaK 18/36/37

The one-piece or multi-section barrels employed on the 8.8cm FlaK 18, 36 and 37 were all 56 calibres long, that is the barrel length was 56 times that of the 88mm calibre, namely 4,930mm. As a result the muzzle velocity when firing high-explosive rounds was a nominal 820m/s, but the actual figure could vary slightly according to the type of ammunition being fired (of which more later), resulting in a maximum possible vertical range of 14,860m. However, the maximum operational range was stated in firing tables to be limited to 10,600m by practical and fire-control factors, although 8,000m was a more likely figure. These operational ranges were, during the 1930s and the early 1940s, more than adequate to enable the guns realistically to engage almost any contemporary high-flying tactical aircraft target.

The design of the gun followed normal German practices of the period in that it had a massive, horizontal sliding breech mechanism with the breech block sliding to the right. Breech actuation could be either manual or automatic. Spent-case ejection was automatic as the breech opened, a fresh fixed round being loaded either by hand or with the assistance of a power-operated rammer from

An 8.8cm FlaK 18 with the L/56 barrel at the maximum elevation angle.
(P Chamberlain Collection)

An Allied soldier posing by the breech of a captured 8.8cm FlaK 36 somewhere in North Africa. (P Chamberlain Collection)

a 'fold-over' loading tray. The tray and rammer proved to be troublesome so they were frequently removed. Firing was effected via a percussion mechanism cocked (charged) either by hand or automatically, the usual firing safeties being incorporated. Triggering involved a lever to the left of the breech and by the loading mechanism.

On all three 8.8cm FlaK 18/36/37 variants the recoil mechanism was the same (although some adjustments had to be introduced whenever the heavier multi-section RA 9 barrel was installed) and operated on standard hydro-pneumatic principles. The recuperator cylinder was located over the barrel, with the longer recoil cylinder beneath the barrel. Both contained a glycerine-water mixture and nitrogen to absorb the firing forces and return the barrel to its loading and firing position.

The gun was mounted on a cradle resting on the two rearwards-curved trunnions, which were, in turn, mounted on a conical pedestal. From this pedestal the gun could be levelled and traversed through 360°, although internal cable connections to the data-transmission dials and other components limited the maximum possible traverse to two 360° arcs in either direction. The pedestal was secured to the firing platform which consisted of a long box beam fore-and-aft, with upwards swinging outrigger arms which were lowered to the ground

An 8.8cm FlaK 18 on display to the public during an exhibition held somewhere within Germany in about 1942. The odd-looking equipment to the left is a Ringtrichter-Richtungshöhrer *(RRH) acoustic direction-finding equipment, while a 12.8cm FlaK 40 can be seen to the right rear.* (TJ Gander Collection)

when in action. In action the gun could be fired direct from the wheeled carriage (with the outrigger arms lowered below the horizontal) but for prolonged use the cruciform platform had to be lowered to the ground from the two-wheel bogie 'halves' and securely locked in place with heavy lever bolts located close to the outrigger hinges. In addition, the outrigger arms were securely fixed in position by splined pickets hammered through slots provided in the extremities of the arms. When the gun was to be fired from a hard surface, or during training on a parade ground, the pickets were replaced by circular or square-profile steel pads. Rough levelling of the arms was effected by levelling screw jacks at the outrigger arm extremities. Final fine levelling was introduced by a pedestal levelling mechanism that allowed a maximum movement of 5°.

When on tow the barrel was rigidly held in a hinged clamp on the main platform cross beam. When the gun was in the firing position the clamp assembly was folded down out of the way. On the *Sonderanhänger 202* it was usual for the gun and carriage to be towed with the barrel pointing to the rear, although provision was made to allow it to be pointing forward. Once in action the muzzle preponderance of the barrel was overcome by two spring-loaded equilibrators inside cylinders slung forward from and underneath the trunnions.

The centralised fire-control methods against aircraft targets have been outlined above, although it was possible to aim the gun using on-carriage fire-control instruments, including a direct-vision optical telescope (the *FlaKzielfernrohr 20*) and a hand-held rangefinder, located on (or in the latter case, close to) the gun itself. This direct-control option appears to have been little used in the air-defence role.

When deployed as an indirect-fire artillery piece the FlaK 18 and 36 were laid using a *RundblickFernrohr 32* (RblF 32) panoramic (dial) sight mounted in a collar bracket located on the recuperator cylinder over the barrel. This sight was also used to align the gun with the battery *Kommandogerät 36* or *40* once it had arrived at a firing position. For aiming at ground targets in the direct-fire role the layer was provided with a *ZielFernrohr 20* or *20E* (ZF 20 or 20E) telescopic sight with range information coming from a hand-held rangefinder, the *Entfernungsmesser 34* (EM 34).

When firing against aircraft targets the usual round fired involved a high-explosive projectile with a nose-mounted time fuze. On the FlaK 18 and 36 the time fuze was set by a fuze-setting machine, the *Zünderstellmaschine 18* (ZSM 18), controlled by a dedicated operator. Mounted on the side of the left trunnion,

Luftwaffe *personnel training on an 8.8cm FlaK 36 emplaced on the Channel Island of Guernsey. Two rounds are loaded in the* Zünderstellmaschine 18 *(ZSM 18) fuze-setting machine.* (CIOS Guernsey Archives)

A Zünderstellmaschine 18 *(ZSM 18) in use with one round already in the machine for the fuze to be set, while another round is ready to be inserted by the K7.* (TJ Gander Collection)

this machine used a light-bulb and pointer display system similar to that employed with the centralised fire-control data-transmission display dials. On the FlaK 37 this machine was the ZSM 19 or 37 and utilised a selsyn 'follow the pointer' system.

Both machines employed a similar fuze-setting mechanism. The nose of the projectile, still fixed to the propellant case, was inserted into a cup in the top of the machine where one continuously rotating set of pawls engaged in a recess in the fuze body. This turned the entire round until it came up against pre-set pawls. When this point was reached the fuze, operated by clockwork, was correctly set according to the latest target data transmitted from the central fire-control position, and the projectile was pushed out of the machine by an internal spring device. Later in the war some FlaK 37 guns were modified to accommodate a ZSM 18/41 fuze setter located on and operating on the loading tray, thus reducing 'dead time', the inevitable interval between fuze setting and loading/firing, the intention being to improve projectile-detonation consistency and therefore accuracy. If none of the fuze-setting machines were operational for any reason, time fuzes could be set using a hand-held setting key.

DATA FOR 8.8CM FLaK 18/36/37	
Calibre	88mm
Length of ordnance	(L/56) 4,930mm
Length of rifling	4,124mm
Rifling	
8.8cm FlaK 18	rh, increasing 1:38 to 1:30
8.8cm FlaK 36/37	rh, increasing 1:40 to 1:30
Number of grooves	32
Depth of rifling grooves	1.5mm
Width of rifling grooves	5mm
Chamber capacity	3,650cc
Traverse	2 x 360°
Elevation	–3° to +85°
Recoil	
0°	1,050mm
25°	850mm
85°	700mm
Max recoil	1,080mm
Rate of fire	15–20rpm
Firing mechanism	percussion
Muzzle velocity	
Sprgr (HE)	820m/s
Pzgr (AP)	795m/s
Max. range	14,860m
Max. vertical range	10,600m
Weight towed	
FlaK 18	7,000kg
FlaK 36 and 37	8,200kg
Weight in action	approx. 5,000kg
Length in action overall	7,620mm
Height in action overall	2,418mm
Width in action overall	2,305mm
Trunnion height	1,625mm
Crew	11
Time into action (6 men)	2.5 min.
Time out of action (6 men)	3.5 min.

Arras

Once the Meuse crossings had been achieved the Panzers were let loose to make their rapid advance along the so-called Panzer Corridor and across north-east France towards the English Channel coast, the intention being to cut off all the Allied forces in north-east France and Belgium. Gradually, the speed of the Panzers outstripped their supporting infantry units to the extent that the Panzer spearheads were virtually cut off from their infantry 'tail', giving rise to increasing alarms at the higher German command levels, which grew increasingly fearful of some form of Allied retaliation against the exposed flanks of the Corridor that would isolate their precious Panzers.

If the German high command had known of the state of confusion and indecision among the Allied commanders they might not have been so worried. The speed and depth of the Panzer advance had not only confuzed the Allies but had increased the feeling of insecurity that severely affected morale at all levels. Allied formations seemed to be constantly falling back to avoid somehow being outflanked by Panzer columns that appeared to approach from almost everywhere.

Something had to be done but no firm ideas arose on the Allied side. They were not helped by severe shortages of combat troops and equipment, a factor compounded by many of the available formations being already in direct contact with the advancing Germans. Communications and movements were blocked by refugee-choked roads, while the *Luftwaffe* seemed able to intervene at will with little response from the French or British air forces.

Nominally the British Expeditionary Force (BEF) was under the command of the French but their commander, General Lord Gort, had his own ideas, ideas that were backed up by his superior, General Ironside. Ironside had decided by the end of the third week of May 1940 to order Gort to attack south near Arras with all the forces he could muster, even though Ironside was unable to persuade his French colleagues to contribute little more than a token level of support to his proposals.

On paper Gort had at his disposal two uncommitted divisions and the 1st Army Tank Brigade. However, the two divisions were woefully under strength, while the tank brigade, which had 100 tanks when it arrived in France, was in the same state. By the time the attack was to commence on the 21 May even those modest strengths had been whittled away by the requirement to garrison Arras and other priorities, such as the need to assist the hard-pressed French. As a result the attack started at 1400 hours on the 21st with just two infantry battalions participating, plus the tanks that had been supplemented by a handful of their French counterparts. Fire support came from two batteries of field guns and two batteries of anti-tank guns. There was no air support immediately available. The attack commenced from the west of Arras and proceeded southwards in two columns, the tanks in the lead.

Despite their modest strengths the attackers caught the Germans completely off balance, numerous vehicles being destroyed and prisoners taken. In their usual manner the Germans soon recovered and began to retaliate with everything they had to hand. Apart from the usual field batteries that included fire from mortars, anti-tank guns, machine-guns, light FlaK and the odd 88. In addition, the Luftwaffe employed dive bombers and other attack aircraft. It was not long before the infantry were pinned down holding ground they would not be able to retain for long, but with the tanks it was a different matter.

The bulk of the 1st Army Tank Brigade were equipped with Matilda I infantry tanks but, thanks to breakdowns and other losses, just fifty-eight were available at the start of the attack, plus sixteen heavier Matilda IIs, also infantry tanks. They were joined by a few Vickers light reconnaissance tanks. Intended to move at the pace of marching infantry, the Matildas were slow vehicles and were relatively lightly armed. The Matilda I had only a single 7.7 or 12.7mm machine-gun, while the Matilda II had a 2-pounder (40mm) gun. However, both were very well armoured, the Matilda I frontal armour being up to 60mm thick, with that on the Matilda II being up to 78mm thick. This armoured protection rendered them impregnable to the standard German anti-tank gun of the time, the little 3.7cm PaK 35/36. Whenever German anti-tank gunners attempted to fire at the Matildas they had to suffer the sight of their projectiles bouncing off their targets' thick armour. As a result, one group of six Matildas was able to wipe out an entire battery of German anti-tank guns without loss. A similar fate befell a 2cm light FlaK battery. At that point many German units started to retire.

They did not get far for Major-General Rommel was in the offing, commanding the 7th Panzer Division. He was able to take charge and organise a gun line made up from whatever artillery units were to hand. This included the 8.8cm FlaK batteries attached to his division, incorporating those of the 23rd FlaK Regiment, which took up firing positions in a small wood near the village of Wailly from where they commanded an area of wide, open, flat fields across which the British tanks would have to advance.

It was there that the career of the 88 as an anti-armour weapon really started for the hastily organised gun line took its toll on the Matildas. One 88 battery managed to knock out nine Matildas, while other batteries had similar successes. Not surprisingly, the British tank units, isolated as they were from their supporting

A scene typical of the Arras attack period with British infantry advancing past a Matilda I tank. (P Chamberlain Collection)

An armoured Sd Kfz 7 towing an 8.8cm FlaK 18 through a northern French town.
(P Chamberlain Collection)

infantry, started to fall back and the Arras attack petered out. By the evening German panzers were joining in the proceedings to the extent that the British activities ended with yet more tank losses. The entire operation had lasted a matter of hours. On 24 May Lord Gort gave the order for the remainder of the BEF to start to retreat to the Channel ports and subsequent evacuation.

Yet the Arras attack had given the Germans a nasty jolt, a jolt that upset their forward progress for 24 valuable hours and which seems to have been amplified as reports filtered up the command chain. Reports were made of an attack by 'hundreds of tanks' and 'five British divisions'. Nervous high-ranking commanders saw the Arras attack as the manifestation of their worst fears regarding the extended Panzer columns. Consequently, the British attack, plus the equipment and manpower losses inflicted, acquired a prominence that by far outweighed the immediate results and made many German high-level commanders even more cautious and hesitant. This uncertainty grew into a factor that was to place yet more operational constraints on the otherwise confident field commanders, leading to the strange halt order later given to the Panzer units on the 24 May while on the approaches to the Channel ports.

The Arras attack therefore made quite an impression on subsequent German operations. On the debit side the Arras attack made the German higher command levels more nervous than they had been before the event. On the credit side the 88 had become established as a valuable anti-tank weapon, a factor that was to have numerous impacts on battles to come.

FlaK 18/36/37 ammunition

When dealing with any artillery ammunition it is as well to remember that it is the projectile that is the gunner's weapon, not the gun. It is the projectile that inflicts damage. In weapon system terms the gun is only the delivery system.

A German listing of ordnance equipment dated 1944 lists no less than nineteen differentiated models of 88mm FlaK 18/36/37 ammunition. When experimental rounds are considered this sum grows further. At first sight this listing appears rather daunting but it soon emerges that the range of types boils down to just two main natures, plus a smattering of not-often encountered others. The two main natures were high explosive (HE) and armour piercing (AP). Of them, eight were HE and seven were various forms of AP (or eight if a hollow charge AP is included – all the others involved kinetic-energy solid projectiles).

All rounds for the FlaK 18/36/37 series were fixed, that is the projectile and cartridge case were permanently secured together so that they could be handled, loaded and fired as one unit. In addition, the cartridge case imparted a degree of breech obturation (sealing) as the sliding breech block employed on the gun could not form a completely positive seal. In all cases relating to the FlaK 18/36/37 series the rimmed cartridge case (*Kartusche*) was 568mm long. Three main sub-types of cartridge case could be involved, differing only in their metal construction. Early examples with the design number of 6347 were manufactured using brass, which soon became a costly proposition and problematic as scarce raw materials were used. A change was therefore made to zinc-coated drawn steel, although this tended to create ejection problems during prolonged firings when the guns became heated. A compromise involving brass-plated steel eased some of the shortcomings of drawn steel and even though this approach did not prove to be completely successful, it was the one that was ultimately adopted. Lacquered steel was also tried.

Corded tubular lengths of Diglycol (nitrocellulose and sthylene glycoldinate) or Gudol (Diglycol with nitroguanidine added) double-base propellant were held inside the case along with a nitrocellulose igniter and a short length of spun lead wire to act as a de-coppering agent for the barrel. A C/12 nA percussion primer was threaded into the centre of the bottom of the cartridge case. The propellants involved were described as flashless but anyone witnessing night firings would have disagreed.

To add to the number of ammunition types likely to be encountered special rounds for use in hot-weather regions, such as North Africa, were marked *Tropen* or Tp, denoting Tropical, the chemically based contents being slightly revised to cater for the higher ambient temperatures likely to be encountered, typically gauged at +25°C (European theatre temperatures were estimated as +10°C).

DATA FOR FLAK 18/36/37 CARTRIDGE CASE	
Design number	6347 or 6369
Length	568mm
Mouth diameter	89.53mm
Shoulder diameter	96.7mm
Base diameter	103mm
Rim diameter	111.5mm
Internal capacity	3,650cc
Empty weight (6347)	3.06kg

HE projectiles were painted yellow with black stencilled markings and were known as the *8.8cm Sprenggranate Patrone L/4.5* (Sprgr Patr). The later Sprgr Patr 39 and its derivatives were virtually identical apart from detail. Two drive bands were provided. Early projectiles used copper drive bands but by 1940 sintered iron (sometimes copper plated) was being employed as a less-costly and less-abrasive alternative. Projectiles provided with sintered iron drive bands had the letters FES stencilled onto the projectile body. The explosive filling could be about 860g

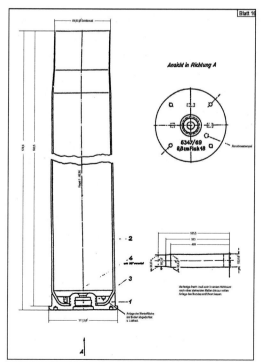

Cross-section drawing and dimensions for an 8.8cm FlaK 18 cartridge case. The cases for the 8.8cm FlaK 36 and 37 would have been identical. (T Parker Collection)

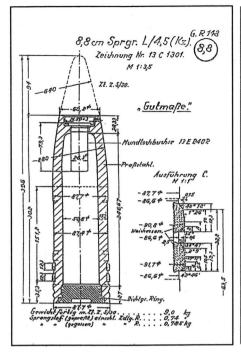

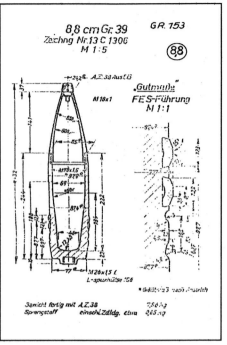

An illustration from a German ordnance manual relating to the main dimensions of a Sprenggranate L/4.5 *high-explosive projectile.* (T Parker Collection)

The Sprenggranate 39 *high-explosive projectile was virtually identical to the* Sprenggranate L/4.5 *other than in dimensions and detail.* (T Parker Collection)

of either TNT/Wax (*Füllpulver*) or poured 40/60 Amatol (*Füllpulver 40/60*). With HE projectiles two main types of nose fuze could be encountered. When firing against aircraft targets clockwork time fuzes were the only type involved, threaded into the projectile nose. By 1945 a percussion element was being added to the clockwork fuze mechanism. For firing against ground targets the nose fuze concerned could be either percussion or time, the latter capable of producing airbursts over a target area. The fuzes concerned could vary from projectile type to projectile type and formed one of the main differentiations between the seven HE rounds listed. A HE projectile weighed about 9.44kg and a complete round 14.4kg. A complete round was 932mm long overall.

By 1945 some HE projectiles were being issued with about fifteen longitudinal grooves, each 4mm deep, machined into the outside of the projectile body. This innovation, denoted by the term *Gerillt* (grooved) added to the projectile designation, was apparently lifted from captured Soviet ammunition, the intention being to improve projectile fragmentation efficiency. If this was so, it was a misapprehension. Subsequent research was to show that grooving the exterior of a HE projectile did little to affect fragmentation – the grooves had to be in the projectile interior to make any difference. As it was, the German grooved projectiles were not issued in any great quantity as they became available too late in the war.

Armour-piercing (AP) rounds used the same cartridge case as the HE (see above), although the propellant charge weight was 2.42kg. The projectile body was painted black with red stencil markings. The base round was the *8.8cm Panzergranate Patrone* (Pzgr Patr), a kinetic-energy round with which the mass and velocity of the projectile provided the energy to perforate armour plate. The main bulk of the projectile body, the penetrator, was chromium molybdenum steel with the same material used for a penetrator cap. The cap, in turn, was covered by a pointed ballistic cap made from thin mild steel, the ballistic cap's function being to add a degree of streamlining for the otherwise somewhat blunt main body and cap. This projectile prompted the British term Armour-Piercing Capped Ballistic Cap (APCBC) in many British intelligence reports relating to these rounds.

A cavity inside the base of the projectile contained a small TNT/Wax or PETN/Wax bursting charge weighing about 156g, the intention being to add to the mayhem once the projectile had punched its way into or through the target armour and also, as a useful extra, it provided an impact indication to the gunner. This charge was ignited after a brief delay by a BdZ 5127 base percussion fuze with a tracer element in its base. The projectile weighed about 9.52kg and a complete round 14.97kg. The overall length of a complete round was 869mm. The time of flight to 1,000m was only 1.25 seconds.

Whereas the *8.8cm Panzergranate Patrone* had two copper drive bands, on the *8.8cm Panzergranate Patrone 39* and *8.8cm Panzergranate Patrone 39-1* the drive bands were changed to sintered iron. All these rounds were otherwise much the same externally, although several minor modifications were eventually made to the base *8.8cm Panzergranate Patrone 39* resulting in suitably amended designations. There was even a variant with a nose-mounted percussion fuze for the bursting charge, but it appears to have been little used. The main change from the earlier model was that the base cavity containing the small high-explosive charge was smaller than before, containing just 60g of Cyclonite/Wax 90/10 (RDX/Wax 90/10).

A more significant change came with the *8.8cm Panzergranate Patrone 40*, also painted black with red stencil markings. For this round the projectile body was mild steel, the body containing a sub-calibre penetrator slug machined from tungsten carbide, with a tracer element in its base. This round was part of the so-called 'AP40' family developed to be fired from virtually all German anti-tank and tank guns. They all contained tungsten carbide penetrator slugs (there was no bursting charge) which offered much in armour-penetration terms over their

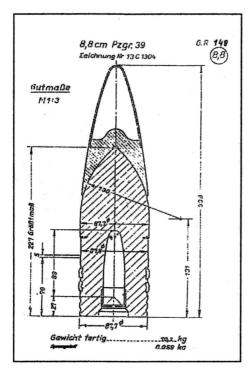

8,8cm *Pzgr.* 39
Zeichnung Nr 13 C 1304

G.R **148**
(8,8)

Gutmaße
M1:3

227 Größtmaß

89

79

27

87,7°

Gewicht fertig..............10,2 kg
Sprengstoff 0.059 kg

Cross-section drawing and dimensions for the Pzgr 39 armour-piercing projectile showing, from the top, the ballistic windshield, the armour-penetration cap and the main bulk of the armour-piercing body. Note the hollow in the body for the base-fuzed high-explosive payload. (T Parker Collection)

conventional solid-shot counterparts, especially at the shorter ranges, as their dense penetrators, fired at enhanced muzzle velocities, could deliver more energy for their weight and size. However, there was a drawback. The main source minerals for tungsten carbide were wolframite or scheelite, to which Germany had very little access, other than from two small mines within Germany that could not even remotely meet German needs. The Allied naval blockade severely restricted the import of all raw materials from outside Occupied Europe, so wolframite and scheelite soon became a critical supply bottleneck for German industry, especially as tungsten carbide and similar tungsten-based products were urgently needed for the machine tools on which all German defence production depended. Almost as soon as AP40 ammunition production commenced it therefore had to be cut back severely to the point where, by 1943, it had ceased altogether, all available stocks of tungsten-based materials then being reserved for machine-tool purposes. What AP40 ammunition had been produced, including the *8.8cm Panzergranate Patrone 40*, was placed in an emergency reserve category to be expended only in critical tactical situations.

An *8.8cm Panzergranate Patrone 40* projectile weighed 7.27kg, while a complete round weighed 13.8kg and was 863mm long overall. The sub-calibre tungsten carbide penetrator slug had a diameter of 35.7mm, was 140mm long and weighed 1.93kg.

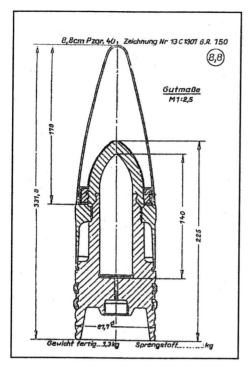

8,8cm Pzgr. 40 , Zeichnung Nr 13 C 1301 G.R. 150

(8,8)

Gutmaße
M1:2,5

170

337,3

140

225

87,7

Gewicht fertig...1,3kg   Sprengstoff............:kg

Cross-section drawing and dimensions for the Pzgr 40 armour-piercing projectile showing the internal tungsten carbide slug that acted as the main armour penetrator. The slug was held in position in a plastic carrier. (T Parker Collection)

The remaining AP round relied on chemical energy, not kinetic. It was the *8.8cm Granate Patrone 39 Hohlladung FlaK L/4.7* (Gr Patr 39 Hl), involving a projectile that relied on the hollow-charge principle to perforate armour. Very briefly, the hollow charge, also known as the shaped charge, seemed to offer much to the German artillery arm as its high-explosive warhead was configured around the creation of an extremely high-temperature jet that burned its way through armour or concrete. This high-temperature jet formation was known as the Munroe Effect or, in Europe, as the Neumann Effect.

By whatever name, as the high-temperature jet was formed only at the instant of impact it remained as effective at the longer ranges as it did at short range. The jet was formed by the forces created by the ignition of 910g of Cyclonite/Wax (RDX/Wax) acting on a thin metal liner that formed an inverted cone, the internal sides of the cone forming and directing the jet forward at a high velocity and a high temperature (about 8,000°C).

When hollow-charge warheads were delivered on non-rotating projectiles they could be highly effective and lethal against almost any contemporary armoured vehicle. However, when carried on rapidly rotating projectiles, such as those fired from the 88mm FlaK series, the projectile spin was such that centrifugal forces dispersed the high-temperature jet as it attempted to form, reducing its penetration performance to much less than that indicated during static trials. In fact, the results were so disappointing for the Germans that they soon allowed the idea of firing hollow-charge warheads from rifled guns to fade away. Any 88mm hollow-charge rounds already manufactured were utilised when appropriate (they retained a useful blast/fragmentation performance and they could still perforate 90mm of armour plate at any range) but they were not much employed with the FlaK 18/36/37 series. Most of them appear to have been diverted to firing from the 8.8cm KwK 36 on the Tiger I tank, which is discussed later. There they could act as a useful general-purpose blast and fragmentation round, although, due to their relatively low muzzle velocity, accuracy tended to deteriorate at the longer ranges. A *8.8cm Granate Patrone 39 Hohlladung FlaK L/4.7* projectile weighed 7.65kg and a complete round weighed 10.65kg. The projectile body was painted grey with black stencil markings, including the identification code HL FES, the HL indicating *Hohlladung* (hollow charge) and the FES indicating the presence of two sintered iron drive bands.

The remaining 8.8cm FlaK 18/36/37 rounds to be mentioned were encountered in relatively small numbers compared to the HE and AP rounds mentioned above. The most numerous of them was the *8.8cm Leichtgranate Patrone FlaK L/4.4* (Ltgr Patr FlaK), an illuminating round with numerous purposes other than just lighting up a target. They were also utilised as aircraft navigation beacons, to denote the location of aircraft targets to night fighters, and even to illuminate sea targets when a FlaK battery was located close to coastal areas. This round involved an existing 88mm naval-gun projectile mated to the usual 88mm FlaK 18/36/37 series cartridge case containing 2.09kg of propellant, the projectile body enclosing a parachute flare body. When the projectile was fired a clockwork time fuze functioned after the selected time interval to ignite a small, black powder charge that generated sufficient internal pressure to force off the projectile base and eject the flare body. After a short delay the flare ignited to burn for 23 seconds as it descended suspended under its 559mm diameter parachute. As it burned the flare produced 375,000 candlepower. An *8.8cm Leichtgranate Patrone FlaK L/4.4* projectile weighed from 9.3 to 9.5kg and a complete round weighed 13.9kg.

Another rarely encountered round involved a carrier projectile with an incendiary shrapnel payload. This idea originally emanated from a Krupp proposal to revive the long-established shrapnel principle, with which a cone of solid steel pellets would be ejected forward by a high-explosive charge inside the base of an anti-aircraft projectile to emerge in a 30° conical pattern from the nose. This idea was developed to the stage where the pellets assumed an incendiary function and were packed around the high-explosive charge. This approach produced the *8.8cm Schrapnell Spreng Granate Patrone L/4.5* but it was destined not to enter service. A Rheinmetall design, the *8.8cm Brand Granate*

Alongside the single 88mm high-explosive round is the wicker and steel container used to carry and store three rounds. (TJ Gander)

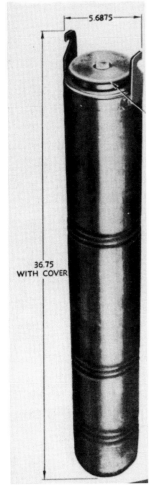

36.75
WITH COVER

5.6875

Patrone Flak L/4.5 (Br Spgr Patr FlaK) was selected instead and was ordered into mass production in February 1944. With this design the projectile contained seventy-two cylindrical metal pellets, each containing a charge of a barium nitrate/magnesium mixture ignited by a percussion fuze. A bursting charge inside the projectile ejected the pellets forward and outwards so that on impact with the target they ignited to inflict the required damage. Once in service this projectile proved to be disappointing. Projectile stability in flight could be erratic, while the pellets demonstrated a high rate of ignition failure. There were plans to replace the incendiary pellets with more stable and reliable explosive bomblets but the end of the war prevented any service employment.

The tubular steel transport container used to carry individual 88mm rounds. (US National Archives)

Checklist for main types of 8.8cm FlaK 18/36/37 ammunition				
Type	Sprgr Patr 39	Pzgr Patr	Pzgr Patr 40	Gr Patr Hl
Weight, projectile	9.44kg	9.52kg	7.27kg	7.65kg
Weight, round	14.4kg	14.97kg	13.8kg	10.65kg
Weight, explosive	860g	156g	none	910g
Weight, propellant	2.425kg	2.57kg	2.35kg	n/av
Length of round	932mm	869mm	863mm	n/av
Muzzle velocity	820m/s	795m/s	935m/s	600m/s

A similar disappointing fate befell another carrier projectile project which involved ejecting a parachute-suspended 'mine' into the path of oncoming bombers. Developed under the cover name of *D-Geschoss* by Krupp from 1940 onwards, the idea proved impractical and too complex for the technology of the time and the programme had been dropped by the end of 1943.

Aufschlagzünder 23/28	Nose percussion fuze with selection for 0.1 second delay.
Aufschlagzünder 38	Nose percussion fuze.
Aufschlagzünder 38 St	As *Aufschlagzünder 38* but of steel construction.
Zeitzunder S/30	Clockwork nose time fuze adjustable up to 30 seconds. Manufactured by Thiel.
Zeitzünder S/30 Fgl	Nose time fuze adjustable up to 30 seconds. Used centrifugal weight action. Manufactured by Junghaus.
Doppelzünder	Clockwork nose fuze with fixed delays of 60, 90 or 160 seconds. Used to produce above-ground air bursts for the long-range field-artillery role.
Brennzünder 8.8cm Pzgr	Percussion base fuze with variable pyrotechnic delay element to allow the explosive payload to detonate inside a target.
Brennzünder 5127	Percussion base fuze with variable pyrotechnic delay element to allow the explosive payload to detonate inside a target.
Brennzünder 5103	Percussion base fuze with variable pyrotechnic delay element to allow the explosive payload to detonate inside a target.
Brennzünder 5103/1	Percussion base fuze with variable pyrotechnic delay element to allow the explosive payload to detonate inside a target.

Inert training and drill rounds were produced for just about every type of round mentioned above, together with Blank rounds for saluting and training purposes. Operational rounds were delivered and stockpiled either packed individually in tubular steel cartons or loaded into wood and wickerwork crates with steel lids, each crate holding three rounds.

An indication of the family of fuzes likely to be encountered in association with 8.8cm FlaK 18/36/37 rounds can be summarised by the following table:

88mm projectiles featured with other calibre guns than just for the base 88mm FlaK series. For instance, 88mm HE projectiles were developed as sub-calibre munitions for the 10.5cm FlaK 38 and 39 air-defence guns with the 88mm sub-calibre projectiles held in sabots during firing – the sabots fell away once the sub-projectile had left the muzzle. Another possible user for an 88mm HE projectile was a field piece, the 10.5cm leFH 18/40 light field howitzer, in which form the slightly revised projectile was known as the *8.8cm Sprenggranate 42 TS*. In all cases the idea was to increase the usual muzzle velocity to enhance range and ballistic performance but, other than limited field issue for the 10.5cm leFH 18/40, the idea does not appear to have passed beyond the field-trials phase.

Numerous sub-calibre projectile experiments were made involving 8.8cm FlaK 18/36/37 rounds. The most usual sub-calibre had a diameter of 70mm (there was also a 72mm sub-projectile programme) and fell into two main categories, discarding sabot and flanged, or skirted. Many experiments were made with these sub-projectiles in conjunction with various types of rifling types and spin rates, nearly all of them directed more towards ballistic research rather than as a direct attempt to produce an immediate-service projectile end product. The sub-projectiles weighed about 4.4kg each, the resultant muzzle velocities being of the order of 1,085m/s (discarding sabot) or 1,195m/s (flanged).

Experiments also included the investigation of numerous fuze configurations, for the German ordnance establishment was constantly looking for ways to reduce costs and improve efficiency and reliability in this area. As a result, all manner of advanced-technology (for the period) fuzes were developed, ranging from rudimentary electronic and acoustic fuzes to photo-electric fuzes that were meant to operate against searchlight-illuminated aircraft targets. The latter development was soon terminated, while none of the proximity fuze projects came anywhere near to fruition.

Tractor

The standard prime mover for the 8.8cm FlaK series was the *mittlerer Zugkraftwagen 8t (Sd Kfz 7)*, the Sd Kfz denoting *Sonder Kraftfahrzeug*, or special-purpose motor vehicle. It was a semi-tracked vehicle specifically designed as an artillery tractor, with conventional pneumatic-tyred wheels only on the front,

A battery of 8.8cm FlaK 18 guns on tow behind their Sd Kfz 7 prime movers during what appears to be a pre-war exercise. (TJ Gander Collection)

steering axle. Powered by a Maybach 140hp petrol engine, it was originally a Krauss-Maffei AG design first produced in 1938 and remaining in production with them until 1945, with more examples coming from Borgward and Saurer.

The semi-tracked configuration of the Sd Kfz 7 gave the vehicle good cross-country mobility, while on firm surfaces it could reach a speed of 50km/h. The unladen weight was 7,950kg, although some vehicles weighed more than this due

The standard intelligence shot of a captured 8.8cm FlaK 18 on its Sonderanhänger 201, *coupled to its rather battered Sd Kfz 7 prime mover.* (P Chamberlain Collection)

An early production example of a Sd Kfz 7 towing an 8.8cm FlaK 18 on its Sonderanhänger 201. (TJ Gander Collection)

to the extra load imposed by added armour, especially around the driving cab area. Each vehicle had seating for up to twelve, plus stowage space for a limited amount of ammunition and personal kit.

While the Sd Kfz 7 may have been a good prime mover for the 8.8cm FlaK series, it was a mechanically complicated vehicle and expensive – each vehicle had a nominal price tag of RM 36,000. The 8.8cm FlaK guns were not the only items

North Africa

On 26 May 1941 Rommel, by then a Lieutenant-General commanding the *Deutsches Afrikakorps* (DAK), wrote the following entry in his diary:

In constructing our positions at Halfaya and on Hill 208 great skill was shown in building in batteries of 88mm guns for anti-tank work, so that with the barrels horizontal there was practically nothing to be seen above ground. I had great hopes of the effectiveness of this arrangement.

Rommel's hopes were to be fully realised.

Rommel arrived in North Africa during March 1941 with orders to organise and field what was in effect a German expeditionary force intended to support the poorly performing Italian forces that had by then been harried out of Libya by British and Commonwealth forces based in Egypt. The DAK were largely made up of a motley force that became the 5th Light Division and the 15th Panzer Division which had previously been based in Italy. Air support was provided for the force by *Luftwaffe* squadrons. Overall, the strength of the DAK was modest, although they could call on Italian Army units to swell their numbers but even so, the DAK was outnumbered by their British and Commonwealth opponents, both in terms of personnel and tank and artillery strengths.

Judging by the number of spent cases scattered around the position, this well-dug in 8.8cm FlaK 18 did a considerable amount of damage before it was abandoned to be captured by British troops. (TJ Gander Collection)

However, all was not well on the British side. Despite their successes against the Italians in Libya many units were subsequently diverted to Greece and Crete, the transfers having a significant effect on strengths and equipment levels among the units remaining in North Africa. There was also a general complacency at command levels for many of the British high-command officers had been trained to fight a conventional war along conventional lines. Consequently, the arrival of the Germans in Tripoli, and the arrival of Rommel in particular, caused them few misgivings as it was expected that it would take time for the DAK to organise and prepare for future campaigning. There was therefore time to plan what they would do.

That was a rash assumption. Almost as soon as he arrived Rommel was rushing all his available units into action (the 15th Panzer Division had yet to reach Africa), pushing through the border with Cyrenaica so that as early as April 1941 the important town of Sollum was taken. This rapid advance caught the British forces completely off balance, despite the disparity in strengths, and by rapid manoeuvres,

This 88 has suffered the fate of being 'spiked' by its crew before it was abandoned to be examined by these British troops. Its shield indicates that it destroyed two vessels in addition to the usual tally of tanks or aircraft. The gun was probably spiked by the usual process of inserting a fuzeless high-explosive projectile nose down into the muzzle before firing another high-explosive round in the usual fashion. (TJ Gander Collection)

Despite the poor quality of this photograph it clearly depicts the urgency of getting an 8.8cm FlaK 18 in or out of action in the open North African terrain. (P Chamberlain Collection)

deep penetrations past the British southern flank, Rommel was able to keep up the attack momentum by attempting to advance still further and 'bounce' the important supply base and harbour at Tobruk. However, Tobruk proved to be too strongly held for Rommel's audacious attempt to succeed so he fell back on his defensive positions at Sollum and the Halfaya Pass. By then the supply situation was already critical for the DAK, supplies of fuel and ammunition having been brought dangerously low and at the end of a long and vulnerable supply line. It was time to consolidate.

During this period, mid-May 1941, the positioning of the 88s mentioned in Rommel's diary (see above) commenced. The British commanders had other ideas. They were well aware of the DAK's difficult supply situation for they had access to the Ultra decryption network, which, by 1941, was able to listen in to German radio traffic in close to real time. In mid-May they therefore launched an attack on the German positions to try and take advantage of the weaknesses of the German formations before the full strength of the 15th Panzer Division arrived on the battlefield (Ultra had indicated its imminent arrival to the British). Despite some stiff fighting and casualties on both sides, the British moves turned into little more than a reconnaissance in force as the German counter-moves were more powerful than expected. The British forces returned to their start line.

The main British response was to be Operation Battleaxe. Taking advantage of a supply convoy that arrived in Egypt carrying nearly 300 Matilda and Crusader tanks, the British decided to launch a major offensive with the aim of retaking Cyrenaica and ultimately driving on towards Tripoli. It was an ambitious scheme but it was carried out with little finesse. On the morning of the 15 June 1941 Operation Battleaxe commenced, the British and Commonwealth troops simply moving forward towards the prepared German positions at Sollum and Halfaya Pass.

A typical example of the fighting that followed can be seen by the attack of the 11th Indian Brigade at Halfaya supported by twelve Matilda tanks (the term Matilda

II had by then been dropped as all the Matilda Is had been left behind in France in June 1940). The tanks ran slap into 13 emplaced 88s, which promptly annihilated 11 out of the 12 Matildas that started the operation. Not surprisingly, the infantry part of the attack stalled.

The Matildas could do little to retaliate. Their 2-pounder guns lacked high-explosive projectiles and all they had to fire were solid armour-piercing projectiles which could do little to damage the emplaced 88s, even if they were able to advance to the effective range of their guns – which few did. As it turned out the Halfaya Pass positions were to prove one of the crucial points of what became known as the Battle of Sollum. If the British had been able to take the German positions as planned, Sollum would almost inevitably have fallen and the German and Italian positions in North Africa would then have been very different. As it was, the 88s played a major role in their retention.

The total of British tanks that started Operation Battleaxe was never finally determined but was probably between 170 and 250. The German tank strength was a total of 196, not all of them useful 'gun' tanks and nearly 100 of them were Italian. By the end of the first day of the battle over half of the British tank total was out of action, many of them victims of those carefully emplaced 88s. Later analysis revealed that one British tank was knocked out for every twenty 88mm rounds fired. Other British casualties were inflicted by the more conventional anti-tank guns, anti-tank mines and by mechanical breakdowns, especially among the unreliable Crusaders. To add to the battle, on the evening of the first day the 15th Panzer Division had started to arrive from the north.

On 16 June the 5th Light Division began to play their part by sweeping in from the west towards the Halfaya Pass in order to cut the British supply route to Sollum and isolate the British forces operating there. That day, and the next, turned into a series of tank and infantry battles with both sides losing tanks and men in significant numbers. On the 17th the British decided that, as they were running short of ammunition and fuel and, having lost well over ninety tanks (some of their early casualties had been recovered), they would have to withdraw – Rommel's DAK were unable to prevent them doing so as their forces were exhausted and were once again critically short of combat supplies. The Germans were left in possession of the battlefield and were therefore able to recover and repair many of their tank casualties, ready for the next phase, the advance on Tobruk.

In June 1941 the way to Egypt was open to the DAK but the North African campaign still had two years to run. The 88s continued to play their valuable part. On many more occasions emplaced 88s were able to halt British tank movements by careful battlefield ploys that drew them towards emplaced guns. There were several ways of doing this, one of the more usual being the exposure of a small force of German tanks that retreated as the British advanced, luring the British armour into positions where the 88s could inflict their worst. It took some time for the British tankies to grow wary of such ruses, for many of their crews were still conditioned by the old cavalry spirit that placed the cavalry charge at the height of their tactical doctrine. Unfortunately for them, such direct tactics were of little value against the long-ranging German 88s.

towed by them for they were also employed to pull medium field-artillery pieces with calibres of about 150mm and, later in the war, some were utilised as mobile firing platforms for 2cm and 3.7cm light FlaK guns.

The Sd Kfz 7 was always in short supply so many other vehicles, both wheeled and semi-tracked, were often employed as substitutes. A typical alternative was the Henschel Type 33 D1 6 x 4 wheeled medium truck. As this type of vehicle was rather underpowered for towing such a heavy gun, it was largely confined to towing tasks over firm going. As a result, semi-tracked prime movers were always preferred.

Totals

When the Second World War began in September 1939 the *Luftwaffe* had about 2,600 88mm guns in the field. During 1938 an ambitious production schedule was drawn up. Until 1938 the production totals had been running at a steady twenty guns every month. Starting during 1939, this total was to increase to 155 guns every month, the intention being that there would be 8,200 guns in service by the end of 1942. The start of the war upset those plans.

Actual production figures for the 8.8cm FlaK 18/36/37 have proved difficult to determine for several reasons. One is that they tend to be fragmented. Some totals referred only to the numbers delivered to the *Luftwaffe*, while others referred only to deliveries to the Army (*Heer*). Some totals include production not only for the German *Wehrmacht* but for export sales or 'military assistance' as well, while others included totals for the 8.8cm FlaK 41. The table below lists not production but in-service totals, and even then they date to only between

1942	September	5,184	1944	January	8,658
	October	5,265		February	8,870
	November	5,413		March	9,010
	December	6,148		April	9,333
1943	January	6,183		May	9,787
	February	6,508		June	10,107
	March	6,673		July	10,286
	April	6,670		August	10,704
	May	6,379		September	9,125
	June	6,448		October	9,639
	July	6,617		November	9,734
	August	7,024		December	9,878
	September	7,269	1945	January	9,442
	October	7,641		February	8,769
	November	7,809			
	December	8,214			

September 1942 and February 1945. After the latter date the internal affairs of what was left of the *Dritter Reich* were in such a state that inventory totals proved to be almost impossible to compile with any degree of accuracy.

If the production totals cannot be readily determined the manufacturers of the FlaK 18/36/37 can. Initial production was undertaken by Krupp AG at Essen but was soon dispersed to other centres. In time, production of the 8.8cm FlaK 18/36/37 series involved a significant sector of the German defence manufacturing infrastructure and it must be stressed that the following list includes only the prime manufacturing establishments:

A O Hering, Neustadt
Gebruder Böhler & Co. AG, Kapfenberg-Deuchendorf/Steiermark
JM Voith, Heidenheim/Brenz
F Werleim & Co., Wien
AG vorm Skoda-Werke, Pilsen und Dubnica
Keuwerk Eintrachthütte, Schweintochlowitz
Friedr Krupp Grusonwerk, Magdenburg-Bückau
Masch-Fabr Augsburg-Nürnberg (MAN) AG, Augsburg
Berlin-Erf Masch-Fabr AG, Erfurt
Masch-Fabr Andritz AG, Graz-Andritz
Ost Masch GmbH, Sosnowitz

Each of the above employed myriad sub-contractors, while others were responsible only for final assembly. The same can be said for what became one of the most time-, care- and resource-demanding sub-components for the guns, namely the RA 9 multi-section barrels. The list of manufacturers for this critical item included the following:

Berlin-Erf Masch-Fabr AG, Erfurt
JM Voith, Heidenheim/Brenz
Masch-Fabr Augsburg-Nürnberg (MAN) AG, Augsburg
AG vorm Skoda-Werke, Pilsen und Dubnica
Masch-Fabr Andritz AG, Graz-Andritz
Gebruder Böhler & Co. AG, Kapfenberg-Deuchendorf/Steiermark
Ost Masch GmbH, Sosnowitz

Carriage variations

As early as 1939 a proportion of the FlaK 18/36/37 guns were being delivered without the mobile field carriage. As the guns involved were intended for permanent installation at prepared and protected static battery positions there was no need for the mobile carriage or the cruciform firing platform, but to transport these 'static' guns to where they were needed a special trailer, the *Sonderanhänger 205*, was developed. Once they were in position the gun pedestals were bolted down or otherwise secured onto a concrete bed. Such guns were differentiated by the /2 suffix to their designation, becoming the 8.8cm FlaK 18/2, 36/2 or 37/2. By the end of 1943 demands on the manufacturing facilities, to say nothing of dwindling raw material resources, were such that from two-thirds to three-quarters of all FlaK 18/36/37 production was being devoted to the /2 carriage guns. By the end of 1944 many static battery sites were being overrun by the advancing Allies, with the resultant loss of their precious emplaced weapons, for there was no easy way of removing and transporting them. In a belated attempt to provide some measure of tactical mobility for the static /2 guns an order for 4,000 mobile cruciform mountings was placed in early January 1945. The intention was that these 'emergency' carriages would be able to accommodate a wide variety of static FlaK guns, apart from the 88 series, but by the time the order was placed there was no hope of so many carriages ever being manufactured, let alone delivered.

The *Sonderanhänger 201 und 202* were utilised, sometimes in a slightly modified form, to transport some of the fire-control equipment that controlled 88mm batteries. One such item was the *Kommandogerät 36* or *40*, while the same carriages could also be utilised to carry large searchlights or radar antennae, such as that for the *Funkmessgerät (FlaK) 39T Würzburg D (Dora)* target acquisition and rangefinding radar often associated with 88mm air-defence batteries. Suitably enlarged, the cruciform-platform configuration was adopted to carry the 10.5cm FlaK 38 and 39. The 8.8cm FlaK 41, which is discussed later, also employed the *Sonderanhänger 202*.

Almost as soon as the FlaK 18 entered production in 1933 consideration was being given to developing a remotely controlled version to be operated from a central fire-control position, the intention being that all barrel-laying movements, fuze settings and (eventually) ammunition handling could be carried out at higher speeds and with greater accuracy than that possible with a human gun crew. Krupp, Rheinmetall and Siemens Apparate und Maschinen (SAM) combined to carry out the development of what became code-named as the 8.8cm FlaK J. SAM developed two similar electro-hydraulic control-system prototypes that differed only in detail and, starting during 1935, both Krupp and Rheinmetall carried out a series of parallel trials, each concern utilising one of the systems installed on a FlaK 18. Both systems tested could be disconnected for laying to be carried out manually when necessary.

The results of the FlaK J trials were such that no service results ensued, although much of the experience and technological knowledge gained led to other, later, remote-control applications outside the 88mm gun story. It was discovered that, due mainly to the technology of the time, remote laying could not be consistently and accurately achieved under field conditions and that malfunctions were too frequent for comfort. In addition, the mechanisms involved could not withstand prolonged vibrations and travelling stresses. The FlaK J project, which by the end of 1935 had become little more than an academic design study, was therefore terminated as far as the 88 series was concerned.

An outline of another project that was not accepted for service, the 8.8cm FlaK 37/41, is given under 'More FlaK 41s' (see p. 90).

The FlaK 36 carriage was also selected to be the carrier for an anti-aircraft unguided rocket launcher designed and built by the Skoda-Werke at Pilsen during 1944. Mounted on the pedestal were sixteen launcher rails, each firing a 105mm, solid-fuel rocket weighing 19kg. The construction of the launcher unit was simple and relatively cheap since nearly all the components were made from angle iron. The layer was enclosed in a metal cabin mounted on the right-hand side of the launcher and similar launchers were under development for ship and armoured vehicle mountings. The programme seems to have been accorded a low-priority rating and it appeared too late in the war to have any impact on events. Only a few were manufactured. Brief details were as follows:

Rocket calibre	105mm
Rocket weight	19kg
Launch rail length	3.5m
Elevation	–3° to +85°
Traverse	360°
Weight in firing position approx.	7,000kg
Indirect fire control	by predictor
Direct fire control	optical telescope

The FlaK 36 carriage was also adapted to become the launcher for the *Enzian* (Gentian) guided surface-to-air missile. For this role the carriage was altered only by the omission of the fire-control and fuze-setting equipment and the replacement of the barrel by two 6.8m-long, angle-iron launcher rails. The subsonic missile, based on the swept-back-wing aerodynamics of the Messerschmitt Me 162 *Komet* rocket-powered interceptor and powered by a liquid-fuel rocket motor, was intended for use against large day bomber formations and had a maximum effective ceiling of up to 16,155m.

Designed by one Dr Würster of Messerschmitt AG in early 1944, the cheap and easy-to-produce *Enzian* was built mainly of laminated wood. It was guided

The 10.5cm rocket launcher developed by Skoda during 1944 and mounted on an 8.8cm FlaK carriage. (TJ Gander Collection)

towards the target formation by a line-of-sight radio link from a ground joystick controller, after which final guidance to the target was under the control of an infra-red photocell in the missile nose. Some versions were intended to have semi-active radar or acoustic homing systems.

There were five proposed models, only four of which were actually built (the fifth would have been a Mach 2 supersonic variant), but of the thirty-eight missiles tested only a few came anywhere close to meeting the design specifications. As a result the *Enzian* project was terminated during January 1945. The missile wing span was 4m and the body length was up to 3.75m; body diameter was 800mm. Missile weight, including four solid-fuel, take-off booster

An Enzian *(Gentian) air-defence guided missile on its 8.8cm FlaK 36 pattern carriage.* (P Chamberlain Collection)

rockets, was approximately 1,800kg, approximately 300kg of which was the high-explosive blast warhead that would have been detonated via an infra-red proximity fuze. The planned maximum velocity was 1,000km/h. The maximum range (also planned) of 24,500m was reached at an operational ceiling of 2,500m.

Tank Killer: 8.8cm KwK 36

The origins of the tank gun that was to become the *8.8cm Kampfwagen Kanone 36 (L/56)*, or 8.8cm KwK 36, are shrouded in legend. The tale usually follows the lines that Hitler, having witnessed an early demonstration of the 8.8cm FlaK 18, insisted that the gun should be mounted on a heavy tank chassis and the project went ahead from that. Or so the story goes – the truth was probably more prosaic. As the designation implies, the KwK 36, a Krupp design, was mooted as a possible tank gun as early as 1936, while the carrier vehicle that was to become the Tiger I tank was not designed until 1941. Initial production of the KwK 36 also commenced in late 1941. Another legend is that the tank gun was merely an adaptation of the anti-aircraft gun, but in truth the two gun designs differed in many respects and may be regarded as separate developments. In fact the 8.8cm KwK 36 had more scaled-up design features in common with smaller calibre tank guns, such as the 5cm KwK 39 or the long-barrelled 7.5cm KwK 40, than with the 8.8cm FlaK 18/36/37 guns.

The internal and external ballistics of the 8.8cm tank and anti-aircraft guns may have been identical but the tank gun had a one-piece barrel contained in a thin jacket. In common with most other German tank guns, priming was electrical instead of percussion, and the breech block had a vertical sliding action instead of the horizontal sliding block system of the anti-aircraft guns. Other differences were that the KwK 36 had a different recoil mechanism and a double-baffle muzzle brake to reduce firing stresses on the carrier vehicle and its mounting, while the firing trigger was on the gunner's elevating hand-wheel, not by the breech block. The two recoil mechanism cylinders were arranged one each side of the barrel, the recoil buffer on the right and the recuperator on the left.

The only armoured vehicle to enter service mounting the 8.8cm KwK 36 was the Henschel *Sd Kfz 181 Kpfw Tiger Model E*, eventually known as the Tiger I to differentiate it from the later Tiger II, of which more later. This powerful tank, weighing 57 tonnes in action, had an involved development history that has been the subject of many published descriptions which will not be repeated here. Limiting this account to its involvement as the Tiger I's main armament, the 8.8cm KwK 36 was mounted in a turret with a full 360° traverse and an elevation arc of from -4° to +11° in an entirely conventional cradle. Traverse could be either by hand or by powered controls but due to the great weight of the well-armoured turret (120mm thick at the front) the controls had to be low geared and

The bulk and length of an 8.8cm KwK 36 still looms over a corner of the Bovington Tank Museum, as does the bulk of its carrier Tiger I tank. (TJ Gander)

were therefore slow to the point of being ponderous, a fact that saved many an Allied tankie's life. Using the hydraulically powered controls (driven from a power take-off from the main engine) it took 60 seconds to turn the turret through 360°. When the powered drive was disconnected it took 720 turns of the traverse hand wheel to rotate the turret through 360°. Another hand wheel to the right of the gunner controlled the barrel elevation, the forward weight of the barrel being compensated for by a large coil spring inside a cylinder mounted on the left-hand front of the turret. During long-distance moves, such as by rail, the muzzle brake (weight with locking ring 56.2kg) was often removed and stowed inside the turret – there was no barrel clamp.

Direct-fire sighting was carried out using a *TurmZielFernrohr* (turret-sighting telescope, usually abbreviated to TZF) *9, 9b* or *9c*, a binocular sight with a magnification of x 2.5. Also provided was a turret-position indicator dial and the tank commander could utilise a stereoscopic telescope mounted on his cupola and a coincidence rangefinder mounted on the turret roof. When operating in the indirect-fire role (an infrequent occurrence) the gunner was provided with an auxiliary clinometer to fine-check elevation angles. Other fire-control equipment included a sighting vane mounted inside the commander's front episcope. The accuracy of the gun, coupled with its flat trajectory and stable firing platform, was such that first-round hits at ranges well in excess of 1,000m were almost commonplace. Mounted co-axially in the same gun mantlet as the KwK 36 was a 7.92mm MG 34 machine-gun, operated by the main armament gunner.

The rounds fired from the 8.8cm KwK 36 were exactly the same as those described above for the FlaK 18/36/37 series, but with the replacement of the usual C/12 percussion primers by C/22 electrical primers taking their power from a 12-volt vehicle battery. Rounds intended for tank-gun applications were therefore denoted by the addition of 'KwK 36' to the designation stencilled on the cartridge case; for instance, *8.8cm Panzergranate Patrone 39 KwK 36*. An indication of the scale of employment of this ammunition can be provided by the following production-total table:

	1942	1943	1944
8.8cm Sprgr Patr	14,100	1,392,200	459,400
8.8cm Pzgr Patr39	21,200	324,800	394,400
8.8cm Pzgr Patr40	8,000	8,900	nil

A standard Tiger I tank carried ninety-two rounds stowed horizontally around and under the turret cage, including next to the driver, although crews often carried extra rounds stowed wherever space could be found. Most (about two-thirds) of the rounds carried were usually armour piercing, including a small reserve of the precious tungsten-cored Pzgr Patr 40 AP40 rounds held back for dire emergencies. Tiger I command tank (*Panzerbefehlswagen*) ammunition stowage was limited to sixty-six rounds because of the turret-space limitations imposed by the extra radios carried.

The number of 8.8cm KwK 36 guns produced has not been found recorded but it is known that 1,354 Tiger Is were manufactured. There were 84 manufactured in

This head-on shot of a Tiger I and its 8.8cm KwK 36 clearly transmits the power of the vehicle and gun combination.
(P Chamberlain Collection)

1942, 647 during 1943 and 623 during 1944, the year in which Tiger I production ceased. The barrel life of the 8.8cm KwK 36 was given as 6,000 rounds so it must be assumed that the totals of completed tanks and their guns followed each other closely. Final gun assembly was carried out by R Wolf of Magdeburg-Buckau, the completed guns then being shipped to the Henschel and Wegmann Tiger I production centres. The accounting cost of an 8.8cm KwK 36 was RM 18,000.

The Tiger I tank and 8.8cm KwK 36 combination was so advanced that when it first appeared the Tiger I was the most powerful armoured vehicle on any battlefield. The gun's power was such that it could knock out virtually any Allied tank at ranges well over those from which the Allies could retaliate, while accuracy was so good that it could often deliver a one-shot, one-hit kill

Data for 8.8cm KwK 36	
Weight of piece	1,310kg
Length of piece	4,928mm (L/56)
Length of bore	4,691mm (L53.3)
Length of rifling	4,092mm
Length of chamber	599mm
Length of piece overall	5,318mm
Chamber capacity	3,650cc
Length of muzzle brake	384mm
Number of rifling grooves	32
Rifling	rh, increasing, 1:45 to 1:30
Depth of rifling grooves	1.5mm
Width of rifling grooves	5mm
Traverse (turret)	360°
Elevation	–4° to +11°
Muzzle velocity	
Sprgr Patr	800m/s
Pzgr Patr 39	773m/s
Pzgr Patr 40	930m/s
Gr Patr 39 Hl	600m/s
Max. possible range	10,500m
Service life	approx. 6,000 rounds

performance. But there were drawbacks, mainly centred around the bulk and weight of the Tiger I. They were of such a magnitude that mobility suffered, especially as the vehicle was somewhat underpowered (by a 700hp Maybach V-12) and consumed fuel at an alarming rate. Tactical travel ranges were limited to, at best, 110km across rough terrain, while any long-distance moves had to be carried out by rail (once the outer road wheels had been removed and a special narrow track fitted to enable the vehicle to conform to railway wagon width limits). Once in action the Tiger I was slow, lumbering and bulky to the extent that its sluggish turret traverse and inability to accelerate could render it vulnerable, especially at close combat ranges, but the 8.8cm KwK 36 gun could still deliver lethal and accurate fire, whatever the conditions. With time, the Allies were able to develop tactics to overcome the Tiger I's firepower and heavy armoured protection by employing stealth and concealment to allow them to move forward to a range or position where their anti-armour weapons could be effective against the vehicle's relatively modest side armour.

Armour penetration

Much of the fame bestowed on the tank and anti-aircraft versions of the 88 rests on their prodigious anti-armour capabilities. Numerous range and armour-penetration tables have been compiled, many of them based on mathematical computation and ideal test-condition data. In practice the armour-penetration performance of the gun's projectiles could fluctuate considerably due to any number of factors which could vary from local weather conditions to the actual angle of impact on the target armour. The following figures therefore have to be treated with caution and used as a guide only.

Outline German figures taken from a 1944 ordnance manual relating to the 8.8cm KwK 36 are simple and very basic. They are as follows:

Range	100m	1,000m
Pzgr Gran 39	120mm	100mm
Pzgr Gran 40	170mm	138mm
Gr 39 Hl	90mm	90mm

The bulk of the tank-gun anti-armour firing was carried out using the 8.8cm Pzgr Patr 39 because, as mentioned elsewhere, the tungsten-cored 8.8cm Pzgr Patr 40 AP40 round had to be kept in reserve to be fired only under the most desperate circumstances, while the hollow-charge Gr 39 Hl rarely delivered its full anticipated performance and accuracy tended to fall away at the longer ranges.

The following table relates to armour-piercing rounds fired from 8.8cm FlaK 18/36/37 guns against vertical armour:

Projectile	Pzgr 39	Pzgr 40
500m	140mm	225mm
1,000m	122mm	194mm
1,500m	108mm	171mm
2,000m	92mm	145mm
2,500m	82mm	122mm

When the same projectiles were fired against armour set at 30° from the perpendicular the results, again taken from German sources, were as follows:

Projectile	Pzgr 39	Pzgr 40
100m	120mm	170mm
500m	110mm	155mm
1,000m	100mm	138mm
1,500m	91mm	122mm
2,000m	64mm	110mm

By contrast, an Allied intelligence report dated February 1944 and related to the 8.8cm Pzgr 39 lists the following armour-penetration performances against perpendicular and slightly sloped armour:

Range (yd)	Projectile velocity	0°	30°
Point blank	793m/s	141mm	118mm
500	746m/s	130mm	110mm
1,000	701m/s	119mm	102mm
1,500	658m/s	109mm	94mm
2,000	616m/s	99mm	87mm
2,500	576m/s	90mm	80mm

This latter table highlights the dangers of literally interpreting armour-penetration data for it has to be stressed that the table presents ranges in imperial yards rather than metric metres so direct comparisons between this and other tables become more problematic.

Chapter 2

Self-propelled

German 'volunteers' participating in the Spanish Civil War observed the first indications of what modern mobile warfare could be like. Although many fronts of the Civil War remained static over long periods, there were times when tanks could effect breakthroughs and confront artillery positions, including those for the 88. It was during these confrontations that the need to get artillery in and out of action in a hurry became apparent. While the 88 may have been highly mobile when towed on its twin-axle limber arrangement, it still took a finite length of time to get the gun into the firing position, during which time all manner of things might happen. A well-trained crew could manage into-action times of about 2.5 minutes but that was under ideal conditions. Getting out of action took even longer.

Somewhere along the line someone hit upon the idea of placing the 88 on a self-propelled platform. The advantages were self-evident. There would be no need for the crew to lift or lower the gun and carriage from its bogies so it could be ready to fire within a minimal time period. The self-propelled carriage could also carry the crew and some ready-use ammunition to allow it to open fire rapidly. These assets, coupled with the effectiveness of the 88 against ground targets, such as armoured vehicles or field fortifications (another tactical lesson from the Spanish Civil War), gave rise to idea of utilising the 88 mounted on a vehicle as a close-support weapon for ground troops.

In August 1938 the self-propelled concept was turned into hardware form by the selection of a carrier vehicle, the *Sd Kfz 8 schwerer Zugkraftwagen 12t*. This vehicle was a semi-tracked artillery tractor manufactured by Daimler-Benz (among others), modified so that the usual crew benches were removed from the rear to leave a clear area of chassis onto which an 8.8cm FlaK 18 could be bolted. In addition, armour, proof against 7.92mm armour-piercing ammunition, was added around the engine and the driver's position, while the gun was also provided with an armoured shield. By mid-1939 ten vehicle and FlaK 18 combinations had been delivered to see action in Poland during September 1939, where they proved to be particularly effective against bunkers. In 1940 six vehicles also took part in the Battle of France where they were deployed as *Panzerjäger* (literally 'tank hunters').

A rather battered-looking 8.8cm FlaK Sfl (Sfl – Selbstfahrlafette – self-propelled carriage) carrying an 8.8cm FlaK 18. (P Chamberlain Collection)

After the fall of France this vehicle/FlaK 18 combination, by then generally known as the 8.8cm FlaK Sfl (Sfl – *Selbstfahrlafette* – self-propelled carriage), gradually faded from the scene. Exactly why is not certain but a few ideas can be hazarded. Despite its bulk and weight, the Sd Kfz 8 chassis was overloaded by at least 2 tonnes and rendered top-heavy by the weight of the gun, while the bulk

French refugees making their way past a pair of 8.8cm FlaK Sfl during the Battle of France in May/June 1940. (P Chamberlain Collection)

An 8.8cm FlaK Sfl in action. The lack of space available to service the gun is very apparent.
(TJ Gander Collection)

of the gun left very little space for the crew to serve the gun once in action. The gun could be fired only over a limited forward traverse angle of 15° either side – firing to either side of the vehicle would have inflicted severe stability problems for there were no stabilising outriggers or any form of suspension lock-out. Gun-barrel depression was limited to -4° and elevation to +15°, so there was no way the gun could be used as an anti-aircraft gun. In addition there appears to have been only limited provision on the vehicle to carry ready-use ammunition.

By June 1941 there were only six 8.8cm FlaK Sfl available to play their part in the opening phases of Operation Barbarossa. The last of them had been lost by March 1943.

At least some of the shortcomings of the 8.8cm FlaK Sfl appear to have been taken into consideration when the next self-propelled platform for the 88 appeared. This time the combination of an 88 and an artillery tractor involved a different gun and a heavier platform that was primarily intended to be an air-defence vehicle having few provisions for firing against ground targets. The gun was the 8.8cm FlaK 37 and the carrier the semi-tracked *Sd Kfz 9 schwerer Zugkraftwagen 18t*, manufactured by FAMO. The latter was a much larger and heavier vehicle than the Sd Kfz 8. Powered by a 230hp petrol engine, the gun and

An 8.8cm FlaK 37 combined with the semi-tracked Sd Kfz 9 schwerer Zugkraftwagen 18t. Only fourteen were produced. (P Chamberlain Collection)

vehicle could travel at speeds of up to 40km/h, despite the all-up weight of about 25 tonnes. As with the earlier Sd Kfz 8 platform, the front of the vehicle and the crew cab were protected by armoured plates 14.5mm thick, while the FlaK 37 carried a shield. The gun traverse was a full 360°, with side-mounted outrigger legs being lowered to the ground to provide the necessary stability when firing. Wire-mesh panels could be folded down each side to provide the crew with a more spacious working platform once in action. The rear of the driver's cab housed racks for up to forty ready-use rounds.

The request for this air-defence vehicle had been put forward during 1942, initial plans calling for 112 units. By June 1943 the first guns were installed on their suitably modified chassis at the Weserhütte, Bad Oeynhausen, ready to be delivered to awaiting *Luftwaffe* batteries, and by the end of the following month a total of fourteen had been completed. All further production then ceased. Again, the reasons for this cessation are uncertain but it appears that there had been second thoughts about the project and that other, higher priority programmes had become more pressing as the war situation deteriorated for Germany.

One further reason for the cancelling of the project may have been the sheer size of the self-propelled platform. An outline of the main weights and dimensions of the vehicle can be deduced from the following data:

Crew	11
Weight in action	approx. 25,000kg
Length	9,320mm
Width	2,650mm
Height	3,670mm
Fuel capacity	290l
Road range	260km
Cross-country range	approx. 100km
Engine power	230hp
Road speed	40km/h

One 88mm self-propelled, fully tracked platform that did not leave the wooden mock-up stage was designated *8.8cm Kanone (PzSfl) auf Sonderfahrgestell*, also referred to as the *8.8cm Kanone für gepanzererte Selbsfahrlafette IVc*. Originally intended as a self-propelled mounting for an 88mm-gun variant that eventually emerged as the 8.8cm KwK 36, there were longer term plans to mount a more powerful 8.8cm gun.

Three prototypes were ordered from Krupp during the autumn of 1941 but no vehicles were actually built. This was probably because of the difficulties in producing an entirely new vehicle for which there was no particularly urgent need at a time when existing equipments were being demanded in large quantities. The weight of the new vehicle was originally specified as 22 tonnes but this later rose to 30 tonnes. Armoured protection varied from 10 to 50mm and was later intended to be increased to 80mm. The main power source was a Maybach HL90 V-12 petrol engine delivering 400hp. The anticipated road speed was about 35km/h, while the crew strength would have been five.

One further self-propelled platform for the 8.8cm FlaK series was the fully tracked vehicle that can be found under various designations, such as *schwerer VersuchsFlaKwagen* (VFW), *8.8cm FlaK auf Sonderfahrgestell* or *FlaKpanzer für schwere FlaK*. This platform embodied many of the features that would have been incorporated into the 8.8cm self-propelled gun mentioned above, but the later manifestation was intended to be deployed primarily as an air-defence vehicle to protect armoured formations in the field. It was built to meet a 1941 specification, the development contract going to Krupp AG of Essen. By late 1943 three prototypes had been manufactured based on the *PzKfw IV* tank chassis and other components but scaled up all round and utilising half-track road wheels. The scaling up meant that the vehicle was wide enough to allow an 8.8cm FlaK 37 to fire over a full 360° traverse arc without needing side-mounted outrigger arms. The gun, complete with a shield, was carried inside an open armoured superstructure, the sides and rear of which could be folded down horizontally to form a working platform for the gun crew when in action.

The first two prototypes carried an 8.8cm FlaK 37 while, in 1944, the third was configured to carry an 8.8cm FlaK 41. There were also plans that other (unbuilt) vehicles would carry the anti-aircraft version of the *Gerät 42*, which is discussed later, while other roles for the chassis were forecast. An illustration of the VFW carrying an 8.8cm FlaK 41 can be seen in the section on the FlaK 41 (see pp. 93–94).

In the event the entire programme was cancelled during 1944. By that stage of the war the German defence industrial infrastructure had more important things to do. Outline details of the *schwerer VersuchsFlaKwagen* (VFW) were as follows:

Crew	8
Weight in action	approx. 26,000kg
Length	approx. 7,000mm
Width	approx. 3,000mm
Height	approx. 2,800mm
Engine power	360hp
Road range	250km
Road speed	35km/h

Yet another 8.8cm FlaK 18 or FlaK 36 carrier was called for during 1940, this time apparently to form part of the air-defence equipment for the so-called Light Divisions that were being formed. (Some references mention that the gun/vehicle was intended to be a mobile air-defence measure for the *Führer* and his entourage during their travels around the *Reich*.) This time the carrier was to be wheeled. Eventually the only suitable German vehicle large enough to carry such a large gun emerged as a VOMAG (Vogtländische Maschinenfabrik AG of

Few illustrations of the 8.8cm FlaK 18 combined with a VOMAG truck chassis seem to exist. This is one of the few that can be found. (P Chamberlain Collection)

Plauen) 6 x 4 9-tonne converted bus chassis. As the gun was intended to be a dual-role weapon the gun was secured on a mounting plate on the low-profile chassis frame and ammunition lockers were built onto the rear of the vehicle. As might be expected, the sides next to the gun could be folded down to act as working platforms. Stabiliser arms could be installed on both sides.

The programme appears to have been given a low priority for by early 1945 only about twenty vehicles had been produced, not all of them gun carriers but enough to equip partially a single experimental mixed calibre *Luftwaffe* FlaK battalion, namely *1 Abteilung/FlaK Regiment 42 (mot S)*. The three-battery regiment (a fourth battery was added during 1943) was formed at Dresden during April 1941. Support vehicles, such as command vehicles and fire-control-equipment carriers, were also on VOMAG chassis. Such was the need for anything that could fire by the late 1944 stage of the war that those few vehicles were sent to the Eastern Front and were lost to the advancing Red Army in the Budapest area. This vehicle and gun combination remains one of the German mystery vehicles of the Second World War era.

Available data for these vehicles is as follows:

Combat weight	19,000kg
Length	10.29m
Wheelbase	6m + 1.35m
Turning circle	26.5m
Engine power	VOMAG 6-cylinder diesel delivering 150hp
Rounds carried	72

Railway mountings

The Allied policy of concentrating its ever-growing bomber forces on single target areas in turn, sometimes for weeks at a time, as with the Hamburg raids and 'The Battle of the Ruhr', had the dual effects of intensifying the material damage inflicted and overwhelming local defence measures. One German response to these prolonged onslaughts was to provide railway mountings to enable batteries of anti-aircraft guns to 'follow' the attacking bomber formations whenever it became apparent that they were concentrating their efforts on specific areas.

These batteries, known collectively as *EisenbahnFlaK*, covering several FlaK calibres, were mounted on several types of converted or specially built railway wagons. In terms of the 8.8cm FlaK, one of the most widely encountered specially built wagons was the *Geschützwagen III (eisb) schwere FlaK*. This wagon mounted a single 8.8cm FlaK 18/36/37 gun on a /2 static mounting. Each wagon had drop sides and stabilising screw jacks. Lockers on the wagon could carry 216 ready-use rounds, with more rounds carried on accompanying wagons.

A typical Eisenbahn *detachment with two guns on a single wagon. The guns appear to be 8.8cm FlaK 37.* (P Chamberlain Collection)

The crews of an 8.8cm Eisenbahn *battery rushing to their guns, a typical sight around many German cities by 1944, although these crews appear to be training in what seems to be a warm climate.* (P Chamberlain Collection)

Although the *Geschützwagen III* was widely deployed, there were many other different types of railway wagon utilised for the same purpose. Some large wagons could carry two 8.8cm FlaK guns, while others were converted from fully enclosed wagons rather than flat-bed arrangements. Also in service were field conversions of 8.8cm FlaK guns still on their cruciform firing platforms but with the folding side arms removed and the main cross-member bolted down onto standard unconverted flat-bed goods wagons. There were numerous variations on this theme.

When in action the railway batteries usually operated from marshalling yards or suitable sidings. The gun crews lived on the train in converted carriages or goods wagons, the train also incorporating all the ammunition magazines, offices, command centres, workshops, kitchens and other work areas needed by any artillery battery. The necessary fire-control equipment was also carried on the train. Many of the simpler field conversions usually lacked some of these refinements.

The mounting for this rail-wagon-fixed 8.8cm FlaK 18 has a somewhat improvised appearance. The side outrigger arms have been removed to allow the main fore and aft cruciform beams to be bolted onto the cargo bed. (TJ Gander Collection)

Ferries

There was one further form of mobile 88 and that involved the Siebel Ferry (*Siebel Fähre*). These multi-purpose, open-decked craft could carry all manner of heavy loads, among which were 88s that converted them into so-called *FlaK-Fähre*. Originally developed to take part in Operation Seelöwe (Operation Sea Lion), the planned amphibious invasion of the United Kingdom, the Siebel Ferry was a shallow-draught, twin-hulled craft. Although intended to cross the English Channel, it also ended up working in relatively calm open waters such as parts of the Baltic, the Adriatic and the Mediterranean during the summer months, all in addition to operating on inland waterways.

The Siebel Ferry was designed by one *Luftwaffenoberst* Siebel, and was largely constructed from readily available combat engineer (*Pioniere*) equipments, the twin hulls being made up from bridging pontoons. There were several forms of these ferries but most were about 22m long and 17m wide, the gap between the two pontoon banks being about 6m. Power from time-expired BMW aircraft or (later) Opel and Ford truck engines could produce a maximum speed of from 8 to 9 knots. About 400 were built.

A FlaK 18 standing by to defend a FlaK-Fähre. This gun does not appear to be a permanent fixture for the ferry as one of the bogies for the Sonderanhänger can be seen. (TJ Gander Collection)

When configured as a *FlaK-Fähre,* a single ferry could carry up to three 88s to provide air-defence cover for other craft or to add to the air defences of harbours. One gun was located on the front of each pontoon bank, with the third to the rear on the decking that joined the two hulls. These craft were usually manned by *Luftwaffe* personnel. The ferries could carry armament other than 88s, 2cm and 3.7cm FlaK guns being typical alternatives.

The Siebel Ferry should not be confused with the so-called *Artillerieträger* which provided off-shore air defence for naval units operating along the French coast and elsewhere. These escort craft, based on barges, did carry two 88mm anti-aircraft guns but they were naval guns having little in common with the 88s outlined in these pages.

Chapter 3

The Rheinmetall Gun – 8.8cm FlaK 41

By the late 1930s it was apparent that the development of bomber aircraft was rapidly reaching the stage where the firepower performance of the 8.8cm FlaK 18/36/37 series would shortly be inadequate to deal with targets that would before long be flying faster and higher than had been hitherto thought possible. To prepare for such a situation Rheinmetall was awarded a development contract for a new anti-aircraft gun with sufficient muzzle velocity to allow the higher altitudes involved to be reached. By the time the contract was awarded (1939) no drastic technical problems were foreseen that could hinder the velocity and other ballistic challenges involved. By then the advantages introduced by the appearance of Gudol-type propellants and sintered iron driving bands had largely overcome many of the problems that might otherwise have arisen.

The new Rheinmetall gun was given the development designation of *Gerät 37* (Equipment 37). The specification for the gun was, for the period, something of a challenge. Having noted the dual-purpose role of the existing 8.8cm FlaK 18 during the Spanish Civil War, the new gun was called upon to have an anti-tank as well as an anti-aircraft function. In order to keep down weight, power controls were not to be employed. The *Luftwaffe* specifications also included the following criteria:

Muzzle velocity	at least 1,000m/s
Projectile weight	9.4kg
Weight in action	not more than 8 tonnes
Rate of fire	25rds/min

Rheinmetall set about their task in their usual brisk manner. To prevent any possible confusion with the 8.8cm FlaK 37, by 1941 the *Gerät 37*, by then ready for its initial trials, had been re-designated as the 8.8cm FlaK 41. At first these early trials involved brass cartridge cases which worked well enough at the time, but in reality disguised future problems. Even so, there were still numerous other

The prototype of the FlaK 41, the Gerät 37, *on the Rheinmetall proofing ranges. The gun shield has yet to be installed.* (P Chamberlain Collection)

Left-hand side view of the 8.8cm FlaK 41 prototype. (P Chamberlain Collection)

Some idea of the complexity of the 8.8cm FlaK 41 can be seen in this close-up of the breech area. The example seen is the prototype, the Gerät 37. (P Chamberlain Collection)

teething troubles to be ironed out. In common with many other Rheinmetall ordnance designs, the FlaK 41 bristled with novel and untried technical features, not the least of which was a barrel 74 calibres (L/74) long with a multi-section construction that involved no less than five main components. This was a carry-over from the development of the earlier RA 9 of the FlaK 36, the overall principle being retained for much the same reasons as before. This multi-section construction was to become the root of many of the troubles that were soon to arise.

By the winter of 1941 many technical problems had still not been solved, but as there was no alternative to the FlaK 41 in sight the gun was awarded a high-priority production status, commencing during the spring of 1942. At that stage development was still far from complete to the point where it was late 1943 before the first pre-production (0 series) equipments reached the *Luftwaffe* gunners. Those equipments were sent to Tunisia, where they arrived in time to take part in the latter stages of the North African campaign.

Their combat debut was inauspicious. A total of forty-four guns was despatched, of which about half were sunk en route. Of the remainder, many spent more time in repair workshops than in the field. All were destined to be lost when Tunisia fell, many of the survivors passing into Allied hands for close examination and technical analysis.

Designed from the outset as a dual-purpose weapon, the 8.8cm FlaK 41 soon proved to be a great improvement on existing guns. It was, however, complex, massive and expensive to the extent that at one stage *Reichsminister* Speer called for the cancellation of the entire programme. However, Speer was overruled, apparently by Hitler himself, due to the first appearances of Allied four-engined bombers that emphasised the pressing need for higher performance anti-aircraft guns. The 8.8cm FlaK 41 project went ahead – there was no alternative in prospect.

One example of the complexity of the FlaK 41 was that the gun employed no less than three electrical firing circuits. One was for anti-aircraft firing, a second came into play when firing against ground (or sea) targets, while a third was an emergency firing mechanism. The gun was mounted on a turntable, which considerably lowered the gun's silhouette, while the trunnions were at the extreme rear of the cradle to permit a maximum barrel elevation angle of +90° to be attained. The piece continued to be transported on the usual *Sonderanhänger 202*, although FlaK 41/2 guns produced for purely static deployments that would not need mobile carriages could be carried on the *Sonderanhänger 203* during transit. To improve the balance of the towed load during long moves the barrel could be pulled back over the carriage. A gun shield was provided for crew protection.

The muzzle-heavy long barrel and lack of power controls rendered elevation by a single layer so difficult that an extra crew member had to assist in the task.

Side view of an 8.8cm FlaK 41
taken from a German manual and
showing some of the dimensions.
(P Chamberlain Collection)

A text-book illustration of an 8.8cm
FlaK 41, complete with gun shield
and showing the gun-laying control
wheels. (TJ Gander Collection)

Target data transmission from the central fire-control centre continued to be via the well-tested UTG 37 of the earlier FlaK 37, but the fuze-setting machine became the newer ZSM 41, located on two horizontal loading trays hinged to the side of the carriage. Each loading tray had a setting head in which the round was rotated on rollers as the fuze-setting mechanism functioned. From the loading tray the round was loaded by a 'power-operated' mechanism, with the 'power' involved coming from an auxiliary hydro-pneumatic recuperator gear. When released, the mechanism pushed the round into rotating rubber rollers which impelled it into the chamber.

It was not loading that was to be the cause of one of the FlaK 41's main troubles but spent-case extraction. As with the original RA 9 barrel of the 8.8cm FlaK 36, the selection of a multi-section construction gave rise to considerable

One of the pre-production batches of 8.8cm FlaK 41s captured in Tunisia. (P Chamberlain Collection)

expansion differentials due to temperature differences inside the barrel. In addition, the relatively large propellant loads involved with the FlaK 41 ammunition created high chamber pressures that caused the case walls to expand outwards to an unforeseen extent. The ductile brass cartridge cases used during early development tended to disguise these problems so that when an enforced change had to be made to steel cartridge cases, made necessary by the growing scarcity of copper, one of the main ingredients of brass, the biggest bugbear of the FlaK 41 made itself evident. Continual breech jams caused by hard extraction became endemic, to the point of ruptured cases in some instances. One early reaction was to instruct the crews to leave the barrel to cool down after every twenty to twenty-five rounds fired but this desperate measure could not be followed once in action.

The only long-term solution to the case-extraction problems was to redesign the barrel to utilise fewer sections. The number of sections was initially reduced to four and finally to three. A breakdown of how this was accomplished follows:

> Barrel numbers 0001 to 0152. Five sections – jacket, sleeve, inner tube forward section, inner tube centre section, inner tube chamber section.
> Barrel numbers 0153 to 0285. Four sections – jacket, sleeve, inner tube forward section, inner tube rear section.
> Barrel numbers 0286 onwards. Three sections – jacket, inner tube forward section, inner tube rear section.

Barrel numbers 0001 to 0152 were cleared for use with brass cartridge cases only: their breech rings were clearly marked with the letter M for *Messing* (brass). The service life for four- and three-section barrels was usually about 1,500 rounds.

The increased towed weight (about 11,200kg) of the 8.8cm FlaK 41 and its carriage meant that a heavier prime mover had to become involved. The vehicle selected was the *Sd Kfz 8 schwerer Zugkraftwagen 12t* manufactured by Daimler-Benz, Krupp and the Skoda-Werke. It was another semi-tracked vehicle weighing about 14.4 tonnes and powered by a 185hp petrol engine. Relatively few of these costly tractors (each one cost the *Reich* RM 46,000) were diverted to tow the FlaK 41. As more and more FlaK 41/2s were emplaced at static locations, most of these scarce tractors were diverted to their prime function of towing heavy field artillery.

DATA FOR 8.8CM FLAK 41	
Calibre	88mm
Length of barrel	6,548mm (L/74)
Length of rifling	5,411mm
Rifling	rh, increasing
Number of rifling grooves	32
Width of rifling grooves	5.2 to 5.4mm
Depth of rifling grooves	1.05mm
Traverse	360°
Elevation	–3° to +90°
Recoil at 0°	1,200mm
Recoil at +90°	900 mm
Rate of fire	22 to 25rds/min
Weight on tow	approx. 11,200kg
Weight in action	approx. 8,000kg
Height of trunnions	1,080mm
Length in action overall	9,658mm
Height in action overall	2,360mm
Width in action overall	2,400mm
Muzzle velocity	
Sprgr Gran	1,000m/s
Pzgr Gran 39-1	980m/s
Pzgr Gran 40	1,125m/s
Max. ceiling	19,800m
Max. effective ceiling	14,700m
Crew	12

FlaK 41 ammunition

The ammunition fired from the 8.8cm FlaK 41 continued to involve the same projectile bodies as those for the 8.8cm FlaK 18/36/37 (including the *Gerillt*, or grooved projectiles intended to improve fragmentation) and utilised the same fuzes. The main change came with the rimmed cartridge case which, at 855mm, was much longer than before to (in the case of the high-explosive rounds) contain the 5.12kg of Gudol double-base propellant that developed the desired enhanced muzzle velocity (1,000m/s). In addition, the primer was a C/22 electrically ignited component. Details of the case were as follows:

Data for 8.8cm FlaK 41 cartridge case	
Length overall	858mm
Mouth diameter	90.5mm
Shoulder diameter	104mm
Rim diameter	123mm
Weight	6.08kg

A comparison of a complete round for the 8.8cm FlaK 18/36/37 series (on the left) with the increased length of an 8.8cm FlaK 41 round on the right. (TJ Gander Collection)

The propellant was again packed as a bunch of tubular cords, each 740mm long, producing a muzzle velocity of 1,000m/s when firing a high-explosive Sprgr Gran 39 pattern projectile – this high-explosive projectile could have either a clockwork time or percussion fuze, as before. To differentiate FlaK 41 rounds for logistic purposes the rounds were provided with a FlaK 41 designation such as 8.8cm Sprgr Patr FlaK 41. This round, the one most often fired from the FlaK 41, weighed 20.4kg, the projectile weighing 9.4kg. The explosive payload was 860g of Amatol, while the propellant charge was 5.12kg of Gudol. By the latter stages of the war some high-explosive projectiles were being issued in *Gerrilt* (grooved) form.

As the FlaK 41 was meant to be a dual-purpose anti-armour/anti-aircraft gun, armour-piercing rounds were developed. They also carried over the 8.8cm Pzgr 39 or 39-1 projectile or, in rare cases, the tungsten-cored Pzgr 40 AP40 projectile. The propellant charge for the Pzgr Patr 39-1 FlaK 41 was 5.42kg of Gudol. That for the Pzgr Patr 40 FlaK 41 was also 5.42kg of Gudol.

In the event, following the North African debacle, the 8.8cm FlaK 41 was retained almost exclusively for the air defence of the *Reich*, where the anti-armour function was rarely, if ever, exercised. As a result many of the gun's carefully engineered dual-purpose features became redundant.

Armour-penetration performance figures when firing the two main armour-piercing projectiles were as follows:

Projectile	Pzgr Patr 39-1	Pzgr Patr 40
Muzzle velocity	980m/s	1,125m/s
Penetration		
100m	194mm	237mm
500m	177mm	216mm
1,000m	159mm	192mm
1,500m	142mm	171mm
2,000m	127mm	152mm

FlaK 41 production

Production of the 8.8cm FlaK 41 was never on the scale as that for the 8.8cm FlaK 18/36/37 series. The gun was too complex and demanding in terms of raw materials, to the extent that each gun had an accounting price ticket of RM 60,000. There were only two main production centres. The first was the Rheinmetall-Borsig AG centre at Düsseldorf, which suffered considerable disruption from Allied bombing raids, while the second was established at the AG vorm Skoda-Werke at Dubnica, not coming into meaningful production until late 1944. No records for production rates have been discovered, the following figures being taken from *Luftwaffe* in-service totals month by month:

1942	October	4
	November	18
	December	24
1943	January	36
	February	43
	March	62
	April	67
	May	41
	June	46
	July	52
	August	61
	November	69
	December	75
1944	January	78
	February	91
	March	110
	April	116
	May	117
	June	117
	July	149
	August	157
	September	156
	October	158
	November	191
	December	252
1945	January	318
	February	289

Despite its numerous troubles, many of which had been ironed out by 1945 (although case-extraction problems persisted), the 8.8cm FlaK 41 was an outstanding anti-aircraft gun to the extent that it could out-perform the larger calibre 10.5cm FlaK 38 and 39 heavy anti-aircraft guns. As far as the defence of the *Reich* was concerned, there were never enough of them, so they were carefully deployed around targets of prime importance.

After 1945 surviving FlaK 41s were either scrapped, distributed as war trophies, or were passed to the re-formed state of Czecho-Slovakia, where they formed a significant part of the national armoury for some years until replaced by equipments of Soviet origin.

More FlaK 41s

By 1942, with the then new 8.8cm FlaK 41 just about to commence production, it became painfully obvious to the German Air Ministry that the FlaK 18/36/37 series would still have to continue to bear the brunt of Germany's air defences for some considerable time to come. Consideration was therefore given to modifying at least some of the existing guns to take the longer and more powerful FlaK 41 ammunition.

Attempts to install a FlaK 41 barrel onto a FlaK 36 or 37 carriage simply did not work as the stresses produced were too great for the carriage to absorb and the end result was unbalanced and awkward. In any event, there were simply not enough FlaK 41 barrels being manufactured for any to be diverted to such an enhancement programme and, if there had been, the spent-case ejection problems would still have been an issue.

Starting during 1942, trials were also carried out as a joint venture by both Krupp and Rheinmetall using re-chambered 8.8cm FlaK 37 barrels having various patterns of muzzle brake. The results of trials involving 56-calibre and later 66-calibre barrels indicated that FlaK 41 performance could be achieved by increasing the barrel length to 74 calibres and installing a muzzle brake formed from an extra length of barrel with two holes drilled each side next to two screwed-on flange plates. This measure increased the overall length of the piece to 88 calibres. Both smooth-bore and rifled muzzle-brake sections were tested, both with an efficiency of 45 per cent. Extra strengthening of the equilibrators and the breech ring was necessary.

Barrels modifications using a one-piece FlaK 18 barrel were fairly straightforward but the multi-section construction of the FlaK 36 and 37 meant that they had to be replaced by a new one-piece barrel. The same 'power rammer' system and horizontal fuze-setting mechanism on the loading tray as on the FlaK 41 (but involving only one loading tray) were carried over, and the UTG 37 'follow the pointer' fire-control data-transmission system was retained. Cartridge-case primers could be either percussion or electrical.

The resultant 8.8cm FlaK 37/41 met its design requirements, other than in having a slower rate of fire, but it was not produced in any quantity – most sources seem to agree that only thirteen equipments had been produced by February 1945, any further development or production having been suspended some months earlier. One possible reason for this is that producing the hybrid guns imposed almost as many manufacturing and resource loads as the production of full standard FlaK 41 guns. There were also mentions of a carry-over of the perennial bug-bear of the FlaK 41, namely spent-case ejection problems.

Data for 8.8cm FlaK 37/41	
Calibre	88mm
Length with muzzle brake	(L/88) 7,744mm
Length of piece (L/74)	6,548mm
Length of rifling	5,411mm
Rifling	rh, increasing
Number of rifling grooves	32
Rifling width	5.2mm
Rifling depth	1.05mm
Length of unsupported barrel	3,619mm
Length of breech ring	540mm
Weight complete	8,450kg
Weight in action	5,250kg
Traverse	2 x 360°
Elevation	–3° to + 85°
Rate of fire	15 to 20rds/min
Muzzle velocity	
Sprgr Gren	1,000m/s
Pzgr Gren 39-1	980m/s
Max. effective ceiling	14,700m

There was at least one other attempt to place the ordnance of the FlaK 41 onto an alternative carriage and that was the 8.8cm FlaK 39/41. This time the carriage was that of the 10.5cm FlaK 39 which, despite its larger calibre, had an all-round firepower performance little better than that for the 8.8cm FlaK 18/36/37 series. Development work commenced during 1942 with Rheinmetall as prime contractor, but the end result was not accepted for service. The main reason for this was probably as previously – there were not enough FlaK 41 barrels being manufactured to be installed on full standard FlaK 41s, so any diversion of valuable barrels for another carriage would have been unhelpful.

FlaK 41 missile launchers

The carriage of the 8.8cm FlaK 41 was employed as a launcher for two types of rocket-propelled missile. One was the *Rheintochter* (Rhine-daughter or Rhine-maiden). For this role the carriage of the FlaK 41 was utilised almost unchanged other than the gun was replaced by a short launching beam – even the gun shield was retained. *Rheintochter* was designed by Rheinmetall as a two-stage, solid-fuel

A Rheintochter
guided air-defence
missile in its
launching position
from a beam carried
and elevated on a
modified 8.8cm
FlaK 41 carriage.
(US National
Archives)

air-defence missile. A development contract was issued during November 1942 but work on the project proceeded at a slow pace so that by July 1944 only thirty-four examples had been test fired. By September 1994 this total had risen to forty-five.

Three different models were projected but tests were still in progress when the war ended so the *Rheintochter* did not see operational service. The length of the intended operational version, the R-IIIf, was 5m and the launch weight was approximately 1,500kg.

Another Rheinmetall missile that involved a modified FlaK 41 carriage was the *Rheinbote* (Rhine-messenger), a non-guided, four-stage, long-range bombardment missile intended to supplement the A-4 (V-2) rocket – the A-4 transporter (*Meilerwagen*) was mooted as an alternative launcher. When launched at an elevation angle of +65° to a speed of Mach 5.55 the maximum altitude reached was 78,000m.

The maximum range was quoted as 218km and take-off weight was 1,715kg. However, of this take-off weight the explosive payload accounted for only 40kg, which meant that the end result could be of nuisance or propaganda value only, yet unlike most other German missile projects (other than the A-4) the *Rheinbote* did see action. It was used to bombard Antwerp from Zwolle in the Netherlands during November 1944. Over 200 rockets were fired during that bombardment, although to little effect.

The overall length of a *Rheinbote* was 11.4m. At its widest point, over the fins of the take-off booster, *Rheinbote* measured only 1.49m.

Mobile FlaK 41s

There was no development of the 8.8cm FlaK 41 as an armoured vehicle gun for the simple reason that the length of the FlaK 41 ammunition meant that it would have been difficult for a vehicle such as a tank to carry a viable combat load, to say nothing of handling the lengthy rounds within confined spaces. In fact, only one FlaK 41 was ever placed on a self-propelled mounting, namely the *8.8cm FlaK auf Sonderfahrgestell* produced by Krupp, also known as the *FlaKpanzer für Schwere FlaK or schwerer VersuchsFlaKwagen* (VFW). This was the same vehicle produced to carry an 8.8cm FlaK 37, as mentioned elsewhere. During 1944 one of the three chassis produced was converted to carry a FlaK 41 on an open platform with fold-down sides that served as a working platform for the gun crew when in action. That same year the entire programme was cancelled.

During 1943 there were proposals to produce a *Panther* tank chassis carrying a single FlaK 41 in a bulky 360° traverse turret, but during 1944 the programme was abandoned before any hardware had appeared, other than wooden models.

The Krupp-designed and manufactured schwerer VersuchsFlaKwagen *(VFW) carrying an 8.8cm FlaK 41. For travelling the side and rear armoured floor plates have been raised.* (TJ Gander Collection)

A schwerer VersuchsFlaKwagen (VFW) in the firing position and carrying an 8.8cm FlaK 41. Soon after this photograph was taken the VFW programme was terminated. (TJ Gander Collection)

Many German sources state that the 8.8cm FlaK 41was not deployed on railway mountings yet photographic evidence indicates that at least one FlaK 41 four-gun battery was mounted on converted railway wagons. However, from the pictorial evidence it would appear that this was only a local improvisation as the side-mounted stabilisers were simple timber props and the overall appearance was that of a hurried stopgap.

Chapter 4

The 43 Series

As a general rule, whenever a new artillery weapon requirement arose it was normal German practice to give competing development orders to Krupp, Rheinmetall and any other concern that might wish to become involved. As a result of the expertise and experience of their respective design bureaux, it was usual for just Krupp and Rheinmetall to be invited to tender. Yet when the specifications were issued for the gun that was to become the 8.8cm FlaK 41 the development contract was awarded to Rheinmetall without the usual competitor(s) being approached. This deviation from normal procedures may be explained by the fact that Rheinmetall came under the control of the Hermann Goering Werke conglomerate, so it seems that political strings were pulled in the German Air Ministry and the *Heereswaffenampt* (HWA), especially as Goering himself was head of the former. In the strange world of the NDSAP state, assuming the responsibility for an important weapon-development project, such as a new and more powerful anti-aircraft gun, could carry considerable political clout, as well as the anticipation of a lucrative production contract.

Despite such machinations, by the spring of 1941 the *Gerät 37*, later to become the 8.8cm FlaK 41, was already showing signs of future problems so it was thought prudent for an 'insurance' order to be issued to Krupp for a parallel development under the designation of *Gerät 42*.

The 'insurance' specification for the *Gerät 42* called for an all-round performance marginally greater than that for the Rheinmetall FlaK 41. For instance, the projectile weight requested was 10kg, while the muzzle velocity requirement was increased from 1,000m/s to 1,020m/s. Krupp designers approached their task with the thoroughness and attention to detail that was their hallmark, to the extent that the ordnance of the *Gerät 42* was designed to be the basis for a family of three guns. In addition to the turntable-mounted anti-aircraft gun (FlaK 42) there would also be a tank gun (KwK 42) and an anti-tank version (PaK 42). All three guns, having many features in common (apart from their mountings), would fire the same ammunition, be ballistically matched and would be manufactured on the same production lines. There were even

A wooden model of a schwerer
VersuchsFlaKwagen (VFW) *chassis
mounting a* Gerät 42, *seen here with the
side and rear floor plates still partially
raised. As the* Gerät 42 *programme was
cancelled this project remained at the model
stage.* (TJ Gander Collection)

Another view of the model of a schwerer
VersuchsFlaKwagen *(VFW) chassis
mounting a* Gerät 42, *this time with the
side and rear floor plates fully lowered.*
(TJ Gander Collection)

plans to produce a self-propelled air-defence vehicle based around the FlaK 42
and the tracked *schwerer VersuchsFlaKwagen* (VFW).

It was hoped that an anti-aircraft prototype of the *Gerät 42* would be
completed by the spring of 1943. The outline details of the new gun were as
follows:

DATA FOR *GERÄT 42*	
Calibre	88mm
Length of piece (L/75)	6,600mm
Length of rifling (L/59)	5,192mm
Muzzle velocity	1,020m/s
Chamber capacity	9,000cc
Muzzle-brake efficiency	55%
Weight of ordnance	1,840kg
Weight complete	7,700kg
Height of trunnions	1,350mm
Traverse	360°
Elevation	-3° to +90°
Rate of fire	22 to 25rpm
Projectile weight	10kg
Charge weight	6.75kg
Round weight	20kg
Charge weight	6.75kg
Type of propellant	Gudol
Primer	electrical

Before the first prototype was anywhere near completed, *General Luftzeugmeister, Amtsgruppe für FlaK Entwicklung (GL FlaK E)*, the technical specifications and policy department of the FlaK arm of the *Luftwaffe*, managed to upset everything by issuing a list of new and more advanced specifications. This introduced the following requirements:

Projectile weight	9.4kg
Length of piece	7,040mm (L/80)
Weight of ordnance	1,920kg
Round weight	23kg
Muzzle velocity	1,100m/s
Round length	1,220mm

This new set of specifications meant that the design fundamentals of the *Gerät 42* (by then re-designated as the 8.8cm FlaK 42) would have to be extensively revised, almost to the point of a time-consuming complete re-design. The outcome was that in February 1943 the entire FlaK 42 programme was terminated – the 8.8cm FlaK 41 had to be accepted as the next-generation anti-aircraft gun. The Krupp design staff concerned were then free to divert their attentions to other projects including, by then, much-needed improved tank and anti-tank guns.

PaK 43

With the *Gerät 42* consigned to artillery history, Krupp attentions could be concentrated on the development of new tank and anti-tank guns. By early 1943 the need for both was becoming painfully apparent, especially anti-tank guns for the front-line troops. The guns already in service, the 'standard' German anti-tank guns by then being the 7.5cm PaK 40, backed up by the captured and converted ex-Soviet 7.62cm PaK 36, were beginning to show signs of inadequacy against the latest versions of the Soviet T-34 tank series and heavies such as the IS-II. For the time being the existing anti-tank guns could just about cope with the ever-growing armoured carapaces carried by enemy tanks on the Eastern Front, but it would not be long before further armour increases would be encountered there and elsewhere. As always in war, the troops needed new and better weapons without delay.

Krupp was able to respond to that need very rapidly indeed. Using the design experience gained from the defunct 8.8cm PaK 42, combined with the tactical knowledge gained from deploying the 8.8cm FlaK 18/36/37 series in the ground role, they had the first few examples of their new 8.8cm PaK 43 coming off the production lines by the end of 1943.

Krupp technicians working with a wooden mock-up of the proposed 8.8cm PaK 43 to determine the final design details before the prototypes were manufactured. (TJ Gander Collection)

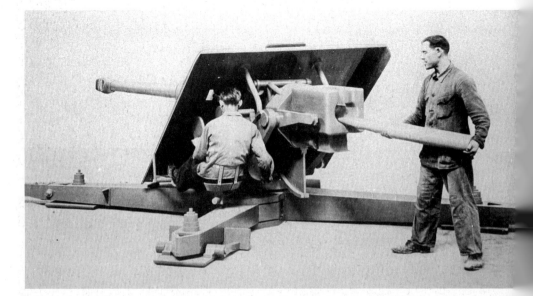

The PaK 43 soon proved itself to be a superlative weapon. Many still regard it as the finest of all the anti-tank guns deployed during the Second World War. It embodied a low, well-protected 71-calibre barrel on a cruciform platform with folding outrigger arms providing a full 360° traverse. Its firepower was such that it could defeat the frontal armour of any Allied armoured vehicle then in service or likely to come into service for some years to come. Yet one of the main changes for the 8.8cm PaK 43 came not with the ordnance but with the ammunition.

While carrying over much the same 88mm projectiles as employed with the earlier FlaK 18/36/37 rounds (but with some modifications, as outlined below), the cartridge-case design was very different. The elongated case approach, as used with the 8.8cm FlaK 41, was not adopted for the '43' series as the resultant fixed rounds would have been too long to stow conveniently and handle within the confines of a tank turret. Instead, the Krupp ammunition technicians selected a shorter and fatter case than that for the FlaK 41, the resultant internal volume still being adequate to accommodate enough Gudol-based propellant to generate the required muzzle velocities. A double-baffle muzzle brake played its part in reducing recoil stresses.

A surviving example of an 8.8cm PaK 43 on display at the Aberdeen Proving Ground Museum, Maryland. (TJ Gander)

Close-up of the breech and aimer's position of the 8.8cm PaK 43 on display at the Aberdeen Proving Ground Museum, Maryland. (TJ Gander)

When in transit the gun was mounted on two single-axle bogies (based on the *Sonderanhänger 204*) and could be fired from them; the road-wheel tyres could be either pneumatic or solid rubber, the latter being on spoked wheels. Such firings were meant to be in emergencies only, for barrel traverse was limited to 30° either side without the outrigger arms swung into place. Ideally, the piece was lowered

A side view of an 8.8cm PaK 43 with the side stabiliser arms deployed but still on its rather odd-looking road wheels. (P Chamberlain Collection)

Frontal view of an 8.8cm PaK 43 in the ready to fire position. Normally the barrel clamp would be in a lowered position. (TJ Gander Collection)

from the bogies and dug in, the cruciform members being held securely in place by splined pickets hammered through the extremities of the cruciform arms. The full 360° all-round traverse was then available. The barrel and cradle were set on a low saddle that traversed on roller bearings. When the gun and carriage were dug in this latter feature meant the overall height was lowered to approximately 1,370mm, aiding tactical concealment considerably. Further protection came from the well-sloped gun shield.

The barrel was manufactured in two pieces. Construction was light, both to reduce weight and conserve raw materials, and this reduced the barrel life to

Detailed view of a captured 8.8cm PaK 43 in the firing position. (TJ Gander Collection)

about 1,200 high-explosive rounds. As will be outlined below, when firing the high-velocity rounds the barrel became worn after about 500 rounds, to the point of being inaccurate unless special rounds were utilised.

One unusual feature for a Krupp gun design was a hefty vertically sliding breech block. The breech was semi-automatic, using two powerful springs that were compressed during recoil to provide a very positive case-ejection action once the breech block was fully open.

Priming was electrical, the usual C/22 primer being involved. A typical example of Krupp attention to detail was that when firing at angles of barrel elevation above +28° cut-out switches prevented the recoiling breech hitting one of the cruciform carriage members. The trigger was located in the centre of the layer's elevation hand wheel. A rapid loading system to be attached to a PaK 43 was under development and still undergoing tests at the Hillersleben proving grounds when the war ended. This system utilised a swivelling drum magazine holding seven rounds, the magazine being manually rotated after each firing to allow the rounds to be loaded and rammed by hand. The system was not considered to be a success.

Direct laying was via a *Zielenrichtung 43 v so* sight unit with a 3 x 8° or 3 x 8°/11 telescope. An *Aushilfsrichtmittel 38* auxiliary sight was provided for indirect fire. The latter feature highlighted a secondary function of the PaK 43 for it had a maximum possible range of 15,150m, which enabled it to be readily deployed as a field gun. By 1945 this was becoming a common procedure as by then the German land forces were woefully short of field artillery to the point of diverting precious anti-tank guns as stopgaps to swell the numbers of field guns available.

British troops deployed around an abandoned 8.8cm PaK 43, while the crew of a 17-pounder anti-tank gun stand ready in the background. (TJ Gander Collection)

The main production centre for the PaK 43 was the Weserhütte at Bad Oeyenhausen, although other centres were involved. Despite the many demands for more and more PaK 43s, production was frequently interrupted by Allied bombing raids, one raid being particularly effective when it shattered the carriage-production lines just as they were about to operate at near maximum capacity. As a result, only 6 complete guns had been delivered by the end of 1943 (although many more barrels than that had been manufactured), plus a further 1,766 during 1944. The 1945 total was 326. Each gun had a nominal cost of RM 26,400.

Data for 8.8cm PaK 43	
Calibre	88mm
Length of piece (L/71)	6,280mm
Length with muzzle brake	6,610mm
Length of bore	6,010mm
Length of rifling	5,125mm
Number of rifling grooves	32
Rifling	rh, uniform 1:28
Chamber length	859mm
Chamber capacity	9,000cc
Traverse	360°
Elevation	–8° to +40°
Recoil	
normal	750mm
max.	1,250mm
Rate of fire	6 to10rpm
Firing mechanism	electrical
Muzzle velocity	
Sprgr Patr 43	750m/s
Pzgr Patr 39/1	1,000m/s
Max. range (+40° elevation)	15,150m
Weight towed	4,750kg
Weight in action	approx. 3,650kg
Length in action overall	9,200mm
Height in action overall	2,050mm
Width in action overall	2,200mm

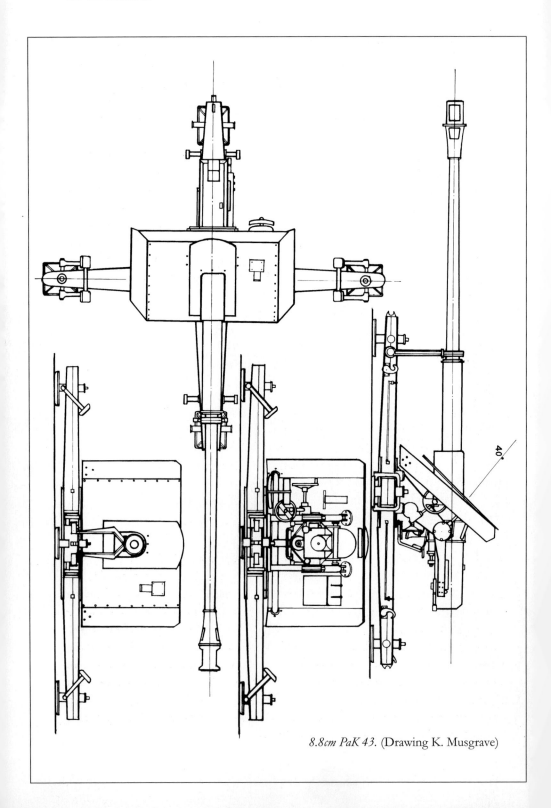

8.8cm PaK 43. (Drawing K. Musgrave)

PaK 43 ammunition

In general terms the projectiles fired from the 8.8cm PaK 43 were basically the same as those fired from the FlaK 18/36/37 and the FlaK 41, all crimped into a brass-plated steel cartridge case, 822.1mm long. A C/22 electrical primer was installed in the centre of the base. However, for the two main projectile groupings, the high explosive (Sprgr) and the armour piercing (Pzgr) there were two further sub-types. The relatively light construction of the PaK 43 barrel, coupled with the strength of the propellant charges involved, meant that the barrels became worn to the extent that in-flight projectiles developed instability and inaccuracy after about 500 rounds of any nature had been fired. To prolong the life of the barrels once they had become worn, projectiles with wider sintered iron driving bands were developed. This measure enabled the worn barrels to remain in service for a full service life of about 2,000 rounds, or 1,200 rounds in the case of armour-piercing rounds, before the barrel had to be replaced.

The 8.8cm Pak 43 cartridge-case details were as follows:

DATA FOR 8.8CM PaK 43 CARTRIDGE CASE	
Design number	6388
Case length	822.1mm
Mouth diameter	90.5mm
Shoulder diameter	105mm
Rim diameter	146mm
Weight	6.08kg

By the time the PaK 43 appeared the standard high-explosive projectile was still the Sprgr L/4.7, as fired from the FlaK 18/36/37 and the FlaK 41, but usually with percussion nose fuzess installed as there was little need for time fuzess in the direct-fire role. For the PaK 43 each complete round weighed 19.3kg, of which 9.4kg was the projectile and 3.4kg the Gudol propellant. These rounds were fired from barrels that had fired less than 500 rounds. Once the 500-round mark had been passed only rounds with wider driving bands were authorised. On the revised projectiles the two enlarged driving bands were 17.8mm wide, the complete rounds being distinguished by the designation 8.8cm Sprgr Patr 43 stencilled on the cartridge case. The muzzle velocity for both types of these two rounds was a nominal 750m/s.

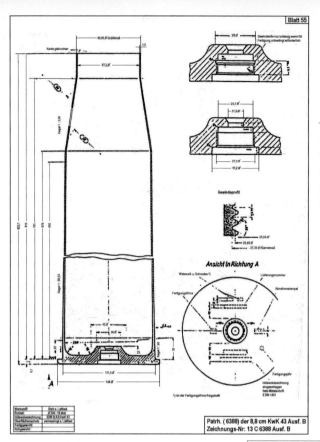

Although this dimensional drawing of an 8.8cm KwK 43 tank-gun cartridge case is marked as for the tank gun, the case used with the 8.8cm PaK 43 anti-tank gun was identical. (T Parker Collection)

Cross-section and dimensions of an 8.8cm Sprgr 43 high-explosive projectile. (T Parker Collection)

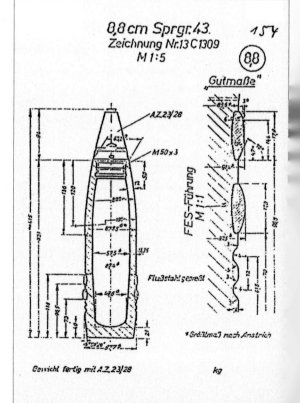

For armour-piercing rounds the most commonly encountered by 1943 was the 8.8cm Pzgr Patr 39-1, which retained much the same ballistic, capped, solid-steel projectile with a small delayed action bursting charge as for the FlaK 18/36/37 series. As with the high-explosive rounds, once the 500-round marker had been passed they were replaced by the 8.8cm Pzgr Patr 39/43, this time with the two sintered iron driving bands superseded by new items, each 16.5mm wide. The revised projectile weighed 10.16kg and the complete round 23.35kg. Propelled by 6.83kg of Gudol, the muzzle velocity was a nominal 1,000m/s.

On paper at least, there was a third type of armour-piercing round, the 8.8cm Pzgr Patr 40/43 W. As its designation implied, this was a member of the AP40 family of tungsten-cored projectile rounds but, due to raw-material shortages, production of this particular round was terminated almost as soon as it had begun. Only 5,800 rounds were manufactured for the PaK 43, all of them during 1943, most of them being issued for armoured vehicle applications, although the Pzgr Patr 40/43 W continued to appear in PaK 43 ammunition listings until 1945. The muzzle velocity was a nominal 1,130m/s.

Shaped charge rounds continued to be used with the PaK 43, the standard round being the 8.8cm Gr Patr 38 H1. Again, this involved the same projectile as fired from the 8.8cm KwK 36 tank gun. Once 500 rounds had been fired from a PaK 43 barrel a revised projectile, with 17.8mm wide driving bands, became part of the 8.8cm Gr Patr 38/43 H1. Propelled by 1.7kg of Gudol, the muzzle velocity was a nominal 600m/s. As before, the shaped charge warhead could penetrate 90mm of armour at any range up to about 1,000m. Only 7,000 rounds were manufactured for the PaK 43, all of them during 1943. Most of them appear to have been issued for armoured vehicle applications, although the rounds continued to appear in PaK 43 ammunition listings until 1945.

An indication of the scale of employment of PaK 43 ammunition natures can be provided by the following production-total table, although not all the following totals would be exclusively for the PaK 43:

	1943	1944	1945
Sprgr Patr	1,164,200	1,115,000	168,000
Pzgr Patr	825,900	1,139,000	20,000
Pzgr Patr 40	5,800	nil	nil
Gr H1	7,000	nil	nil

Inert training and drill rounds were produced for just about every type of round mentioned above, together with Blank rounds for saluting and training purposes.

PaK 43 armour penetration

One German reference provides just two examples of the armour penetration to be expected when firing standard armour-piercing projectiles at a muzzle velocity of 1,000m/s. They are as follows:

Range	Penetration
100m	203mm
1,000m	165mm

The inference from such brief notes is that they were intended as a rough guide only. As mentioned elsewhere, armour-penetration performances remain subject to many variables such as the degree of wear in the barrel bore, the angle of incidence against the target armour, and so on. One generally accepted guide table for armour-piercing projectiles (including the scarcely used AP40 pattern round) fired against vertical armour follows:

	Pzgr Patr 39-1	Pzgr Patr 40/43 W
500m	205mm	270mm
1,000m	186mm	233mm
1,500m	170mm	205mm
2,000m	154mm	175mm
2,500m	140mm	147mm

KwK 43

The development of the tank-mounted 8.8cm KwK 43 closely followed that for the PaK 43 as both were based around their equivalents developed as part of the *Gerät 42* programme, in this case the 8.8cm KwK 42. Only one armoured combat vehicle carried the KwK 43, the *Sd Kfz 182 Tiger II (Ausf B)*, known to the Allies as the 'King' or 'Royal Tiger'. The Germans knew it as the *Königstiger* ('King tiger'). The KwK 43 was also intended for installation in the *Schmalturm (Gerät 710)* of the *Panther II*, a tank destined never to pass the component prototype stage.

Ballistically and in armour-penetration terms the 8.8cm KwK 43 was identical to the PaK 43 and fired the same ammunition. The KwK 43 also carried over the same barrel-wear shortcomings as the PaK 43 and therefore had to be supplied with the same wider driving band types of ammunition after 500 rounds had been fired. The KwK 43 differed from the PaK 43 anti-tank gun only in having

American troops examining a captured Tiger II with the 8.8cm KwK 43 main gun well in evidence. (US National Archives)

the two recoil cylinders mounted over the barrel and being marginally longer. The vertically sliding breech block was also carried over from the PaK 43.

At first it was intended to install a 105mm or even a 150mm gun on the Tiger II, but Hitler once again used his 'intuition' to intervene. He insisted on the installation of the 8.8cm KwK 43, the result being what many observers of the

One of the few examples of the Schmallturm *turret for the* Panther II *tank that was intended to carry an 8.8cm KwK 43 as its main armament. The bulge on the side of the turret is an armoured cover for a rangefinder, the other side of the turret having a similar bulge.* (TJ Gander Collection)

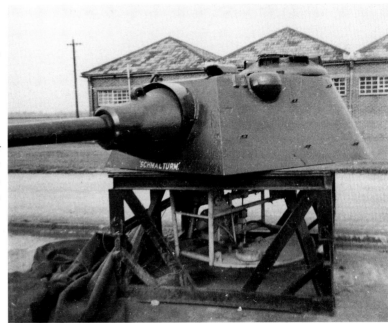

armoured warfare scene believe was the most powerful tank in service during the Second World War.

The KwK 43 was mounted 80mm to the right of the turret centre line in the Tiger II's 360° traverse turret. Two patterns of turret, the Porsche and the Henschel, were produced with slightly different gun mountings. The first fifty vehicles manufactured carried the Porsche turret but thereafter the easier to manufacture and better protected Henschel turret became the main production version. The Porsche turret carried a gun with a monobloc construction. By contrast the Henschel turret gun had a two-piece barrel constructed along lines similar to those of the PaK 43. Both barrel types had a double-baffle muzzle brake. In addition, the Henschel turret had a large cast mantlet of the type known as the *Saukopfblende* ('Pig's Head') protecting the gun and turret mantlet. Stowed in the rear turret bulge were 22 ready use rounds (11 each side) with a further 48 rounds stowed in protective steel panniers along each side of the hull. A further ten rounds were carried loose in various locations, making a combat load of eighty rounds in all. Command tanks (*Panzerbefehleswagen*) had their ammunition load reduced to sixty-three rounds as some of the ammunition stowage space was taken over by the necessary extra radios. The usual ammunition allocation was supposed to be split 40 HE and 40 AP, but this mix could be varied according to the mission.

For aiming, the gunner was provided with a standard TZF 9d or 9bl monocular sight unit and there was the option of powered or manual traverse controls. To overcome the barrel weight during elevation movements, a hydro-pneumatic cylinder was located between the recoil cylinders and the mounting.

The Tiger II first saw service on the Eastern Front during early 1944 and soon established itself as a formidable opponent. However, it had one serious shortcoming. Despite the vehicle's combat weight of 68.7 tonnes, it was powered by the same 700hp V-12 Maybach engine as the 56-tonne Tiger I. If the Tiger I was a ponderous performer, the Tiger II was even more so, to the extent that mobility was severely impaired. Due to the stresses imposed on the engine, drive train and many other components, the Tiger II was prone to frequent breakdowns, while the fuel consumption was prodigious during a period when Germany's fuel-supply situation was becoming increasingly precarious. Even so, the Tiger II remained a formidable fighting machine until the end and often survived due to its lavishly supplied armour. The sloping front hull armour was 150mm thick, while the turret frontal armour was 180mm thick and further protected by the cast *Saukopfblende* mantlet. By late 1944 the Tiger II had become more of a mobile defensive measure rather than an aggressive combat vehicle.

Manufacturing the Tiger II was a major undertaking, demanding in terms of raw materials, manufacturing resources and skilled manpower, all increasingly diminishing by the end of 1944. Just one Tiger II was manufactured during 1943.

A further 376 were manufactured during 1944, plus another 112 before the war ended in 1945. The main Tiger II production centres were at the Henschel and Wegmann facilities at Kassel, both sites being frequently visited by Allied bombers, with armour and other components coming from the Skoda-Werke at Pilsen, Dortmund Hoerd-Hütte-Verein at Dortmund and Krupp AG of Essen. Needless to say, there were many other contributors, not the least of them being Fr Garny of Frankfurt/Main and R Wolf of Magdeberg-Buchau, which between them supplied the main armament, the 8.8cm KwK 43. The exact number of guns supplied has not been found recorded but is believed to be considerably more than the number of Tiger II tanks produced. A single gun had a nominal cost of RM 21,000.

By the time the war was in its final stages more 8.8cm KwK 43 guns were being completed than Tiger IIs on which to mount them. Such was the need for anti-tank defences by that stage of the war that it became an established practice

DATA FOR 8.8CM KwK 43	
Calibre	88mm
Length of piece (L/71)	6,280mm
Length of bore	6,038.5mm
Length of rifling	5,179mm
Number of rifling grooves	32
Rifling	rh, uniform, 1:28
Weight complete	1,690kg
Length of chamber	859.5mm
Chamber capacity	9,000cc
Traverse (turret)	360°
Elevation	–8° to +15°
Rate of fire	6 to10rpm
Firing mechanism	electrical
Muzzle velocity	
Sprgr Patr 43	750m/s
Pzgr Patr 39/43	1,000m/s
Max. range (+15° elevation)	9,350m

to mount some of these surplus tank guns statically on steel frames imparting only a limited degree of barrel traverse when set into concrete bases emplaced in the *Westwall* fortifications (fifty guns were assigned to this role, although not all of them were actually emplaced) or to cover important strategic points such as river crossings. Many of these guns ended up on locally improvised static mountings on rough timber bases.

During early 1945 an attempt was made to boost the performance of the KwK 43 by extending the existing 71-calibre ordnance to a length of 105 calibres. Some design work was initiated but the project was destined never to reach the hardware stage. In addition to the end of the war intervening, a high-level decision was made to abandon further high-velocity tank-gun (and anti-tank gun) development in favour of simpler and less costly smooth-bore anti-armour guns and launchers, delivering finned projectiles housing shaped charge warheads. Needless to say, such an over-ambitious programme never even got underway.

Stopgap: 8.8cm PaK 43/41

When the need arose for a more powerful anti-tank gun for the hard-pressed front-line troops on the Eastern Front the 8.8cm PaK 43 was the result. Krupp was quick to get their new design into production but almost as soon as series manufacture was getting under way in the late summer of 1943, an Allied bombing raid virtually demolished the carriage-production facilities to the extent

Side-on view of an 8.8cm PaK 43/41.
(P Chamberlain Collection)

Details of the breech of the 8.8cm PaK 43/41 on display at the Bovington Tank Museum. (TJ Gander)

that they had to be re-established virtually from scratch. The barrel production line remained in being and continued to churn out finished barrels but there was nothing to mount them on.

By that time, late 1943, formation commanders on all fronts were insistent that they could not cope without the defensive firepower promised by the PaK 43, so strident demands flowed into the Krupp works with growing clamour. Finished barrels were to hand so some alternative carriage arrangement had to be found rapidly. One early expedient was thought to be to mount

Rear view of an 8.8cm PaK 43/41 ready for towing. This example is on display at Aberdeen Proving Ground Museum, Maryland. (TJ Gander)

An 8.8cm Pak 43/41 displaying its hitting power on a training range – the target T-34 tank was unlikely to expose itself so conveniently under operational conditions. (P Chamberlain Collection)

the 88mm barrels on captured Soviet 152mm howitzer or French 155mm GPF gun carriages, but the results were clumsy, heavy and far from satisfactory so they were duly rejected for service. (Both types of carriage were used later in the war as makeshifts for the large and heavy 12.8cm PaK 44 ordnance when there was no other alternative.) The eventual solution emerged as a hodgepodge of bits and pieces of existing German field-artillery carriages. The end result was far from satisfactory but it was available and it worked.

The gun remained much the same as that for the 8.8cm PaK 43, although the breech mechanism, being placed on a cradle and saddle different from those on the original PaK 43, had to revert to the horizontal sliding block configuration, the breech block sliding to the left. In appearance and operation the breech mechanism resembled a scaled-up version of that on the 7.5cm PaK 40. The semi-automatic spent-case-ejection mechanism was also simplified. The slightly modified basic cradle and carriage was taken from the 10.5cm leFH 18 light field howitzer, then just going out of production in favour of the 10.5cm leFH 18/40 which was based around the lighter carriage of the 7.5 m PaK 40. Also taken from the 10.5cm leFH 18 were the box-section split trail legs, while the entire improvisation travelled on, and was fired from, the large road wheels of the 15cm sFH 18 field howitzer. To round things off, a new shield was installed and provision was made for dial sights to enable the piece to be utilised as a field gun (or coast-defence gun) when necessary. The dial sight was the Rbl 32 or 36 mounted over the usual direct-laying telescope.

The end result, designated the 8.8cm PaK 43/41 but generally known to the troops as the *Scheuntor* ('Barn Door'), looked, and was, high, clumsy and muzzle-heavy. Moving the unbalanced piece even a short distance required a powerful prime mover or a great deal of manual labour. The weight of the improvised carriage of the PaK 43/41 was such that it had a tendency to sink into soft ground when fired. To help to overcome this tendency the Skoda-Werke of Pilsen developed a light pedestal mount to secure under the carriage axle to spread the weight over a greater ground surface area. It was known as the *Scheissstutze für PaK-Geräte und leichte Feldgeschütze*. As the designation implied, the device was also intended for use with the 7.5cm PaK 40, 10.5cm leFH 18 and 10.5cm leFH 18/40 as well as with the 8.8 m PaK 43/41.

The 8.8cm PaK 43/41 improvisation had the sole saving grace that it worked when it was needed. A total of 1,403 were thrown together at various production centres during 1943 and 1944 and hastened to the front lines. As the PaK 43/41 fired the same ammunition as the PaK 43 it was every bit as effective as the custom-built gun and the armour-penetration results were identical. The problems arose when the piece had to be moved in a hurry. Many became

DATA FOR 8.8CM PAK 43/41	
Calibre	88mm
Length of piece (L/71)	6,280mm
Length with muzzle brake	6,610mm
Length of bore	6,010mm
Length of rifling	5,125mm
Number of rifling grooves	32
Rifling	rh, uniform 1:28
Chamber length	859mm
Chamber capacity	9,000cc
Traverse	56°
Elevation	–5° to +38°
Recoil	
normal	680mm
max.	720mm
Rate of fire	6 to10rpm
Firing mechanism	electrical
Muzzle velocity	
Sprgr Gren 43	750m/s
Pzgr Gren 39/1	1,000m/s
Max. range (+38° elevation)	approx. 15,000m
Weight in action	approx. 4,380kg
Length overall	9,144mm
Height in action overall	1,981mm
Width in action overall	2,527mm

casualties because they could not be hauled out of harm's way quickly enough, so losses were often high. Yet for all their shortcomings there were never enough to hand for the hard-pressed German front-line troops.

Some German references mention that the gun carried by the self-propelled *Nashorn* was the 8.8cm PaK 43/41. Some of the barrels involved were indeed earmarked for use on the towed PaK 43/41 but were instead diverted to the *Nashorn* production lines (see below).

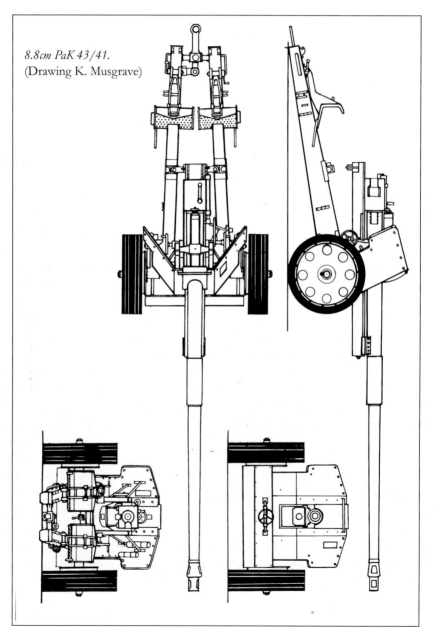

8.8cm PaK 43/41.
(Drawing K. Musgrave)

PaK 43: self-propelled

Soon after its tentative introduction into service at the end of 1943, the 8.8cm PaK 43 went 'mobile' in some numbers on a variety of armoured vehicle chassis. In order to suit the wide variety of mountings likely to be encountered the specialised mountings were identified by addition of a sub-type to the designation, typical being 8.8cm PaK 43/1. The vehicles involved were:

> *8.8cm PaK 43/1 auf Panzerjäger III/IV (Nashorn) Sd Kfz 164*
> *8.8cm Pak 43/2 auf Panzerjäger Tiger P (Elefant) Sd Kfz 184*
> *8.8cm Pak 43/3 auf Panzerjäger Panther (Jagdpanther) Sd Kfz 173*
> *8.8cm PaK 43/3 auf Selbstfahrlafette 38(d)*
> *8.8cm Pak 43/3 auf Panzerjäger 38(t)*
> *8.8cm PaK 43/3 auf Krupp/Steyr Selbstfahrlafette 38(d)*
> *8.8cm Pak 43/3 auf Panzerjäger Tiger ausf B (Jagdtiger) Sd Kfz 186*

Starting from the top of this check-list, the *Nashorn* ('Rhinoceros'), later renamed as the *Hornisse* ('Hornet'), shared its chassis and superstructure with the *Hummel* ('Bumble Bee'), a self-propelled carrier for the 15cm sFH 18 field howitzer. By contrast with its self-propelled artillery platform counterpart, the *Nashorn* could be regarded as an interim solution *(zwischenlösung) Panzerjäger*, or tank hunter, until more specialised vehicles became available. The *Panzerjäger* concept may be regarded as a typical German innovation whereby self-propelled anti-tank guns could be used to stalk, ambush and knock out enemy armoured vehicles and then beat a hasty retreat. Their format was such that their main armament traverse angle was confined to a limited frontal arc. In addition, they were lightly armoured and were not intended for stand-up battles with other armoured vehicles. They were specialised tank killers, not tanks.

The *Nashorn* was built on a chassis utilising many *Panzer IV* medium tank components, including a lengthened hull, but with a *PzKpfw III* final drive. The 8.8cm PaK 43/1 mounting was positioned behind a lightly armoured and open-topped superstructure located towards the rear of the vehicle. Designed during 1942, the *Nashorn* was rather high and heavy for its assigned task but they saw extensive service – 494 out of a planned 500 were manufactured, final assembly being completed by the Deutsche Eisenwerke at Teplitz-Schönau between early 1943 and March 1945. Some German references mention that the gun carried by the *Nashorn* was the 8.8cm PaK 43/41. Some of the barrels used were indeed earmarked for use with the towed PaK 43/41 but were instead diverted to the *Nashorn* production lines. A total of 543 PaK 43/1 or PaK 43/41 guns were manufactured specifically for the *Nashorn*. Both guns would have demonstrated identical ballistic and armour-penetration performances.

A Nashorn *('Rhinoceros') commander receiving a written message in time-honoured style on the Eastern Front.* (P Chamberlain Collection)

The *Nashorn* weighed approximately 24 tonnes in combat and carried a crew of 4 or 5, at least 3 of whom were needed to serve the gun. Maximum speed on roads was 40km/h. Stowage was provided for forty rounds for the 8.8cm PaK 43/1, which had a total barrel traverse of 30° and an elevation arc of from -5° to +20°. A 7.92mm machine-gun was carried for local defence.

Loading a round into the breech of an 8.8cm PaK 43/41 pattern gun on a Nashorn. *Note that the sliding breech block is horizontal rather than vertical, as on a standard PaK 43.* (P Chamberlain Collection)

Originally known as the Ferdinand, *the* 8.8cm PaK 43/2 auf Panzerjäger Tiger P (Elefant) Sd Kfz 184 *had a troubled service career but was a powerful tank killer.* (P Chamberlain Collection)

Next in the check-list comes the *8.8cm Pak 43/2 auf Panzerjäger Tiger P (Elefant) Sd Kfz 184*, also known as the *Ferdinand*. This vehicle gained an unfortunate reputation, which may not have been entirely unwarranted but because of its 8.8cm PaK 43/2 main gun it was a formidable tank killer. The *Elefant* chassis was originally developed for the *VK 4501 Tiger (P)* heavy tank prototypes. This complicated Porsche design never saw production as a tank as the production contract it was intended for was instead awarded to Henschel, which produced the Tiger I. In order not to waste the effort put into the Tiger (P) project, between April and May 1943 the chassis and hulls were hastily converted into self-propelled platforms for the 8.8cm PaK 43/2, initially, it was thought, to be utilised as heavy *Panzerjäger*. Unfortunately, they became regarded as 'break-through' *Sturmgeschutz* (assault gun) spearheads for the forthcoming Kursk offensive, so some user formation reports then re-designated the gun as the *8.8cm Sturmkanone 43/1*. Yet the gun remained the same PaK 43/2.

When it eventually went into action during the Kursk Salient battles the vehicle, then named the *Ferdinand*, was still largely undeveloped and many of its features were untried. It utilised (for then) an advanced form of drive where the two main petrol engines, located in the centre of the hull, developed 530hp to drive electrical generators to power electrical motors coupled to the final drive assemblies. While this drive system could work, it constantly proved to be underpowered and troublesome in service and, during manufacture, called for a

Once the surviving Elefants *had been sent to Italy it was soon found that the local terrain and Allied activities meant that most came to an unfortunate end, as did the example seen here disabled in an Italian village.* (US National Archives)

considerable amount of scarce copper for all the generators and their associated wiring. Matters were not helped by the vehicle's combat weight gradually climbing to about 68 tonnes, which did little to assist mobility. Once in action the absence of any form of close-in defence meant that they became highly vulnerable to the activities of Soviet close-in tank-killer infantry squads.

Of the ninety vehicles converted to *Ferdinand* standard, eighty-nine took part in the Kursk fighting. About half of these became casualties during the early phases of the battle, although many of them were later recovered (with difficulty as they were so heavy) and repaired and used to fight on. One account mentions that over 200 Soviet tanks had been knocked out by *Ferdinand* units by the time the initial Kursk fighting was over, and the *Ferdinands* were frequently deployed successfully as emergency stopgaps to stem attempted Soviet armour breakthroughs.

After the Kursk Salient fighting the remaining *Ferdinands* fought on throughout the summer of 1943. In November of that year the forty-eight survivors were withdrawn for extensive rebuilds, which included the installation of two secondary defensive machine-guns. The *Ferdinand* then became the *Elefant* and all the rebuilt vehicles were diverted to Italy where the unsuitable roads and terrain took their toll, to say nothing of breakdowns and Allied actions. By the end of the war only four were left and they were assigned to the final defence of Berlin, which they did not survive.

Initial production of the *Ferdinand* was carried out at the Nibelungwerke at St Valentin and later by Alkett of Berlin-Spandau. The gun was finally assembled at the Dortmund-Hoerder-Hüttenverein Werke at Lippstadt. Much of the

The 8.8cm Pak 43/3 auf Panzerjäger Panther (Jagdpanther) Sd Kfz 173 *turned out to be a superlative* Panzerjäger, *which became greatly feared by Allied tank crews.* (P Chamberlain Collection)

vehicle's combat weight of 68 tonnes was down to the heavy armour protection, which was up to 200mm for the superstructure front. By contrast the side armour was limited to 80mm. In action the crew was six and fifty 88mm rounds were carried. Barrel traverse was 28° and elevation from -8° to +14°. Road speed was limited to 30km/h. When travelling over roads the operational range was limited to 150km, even though the fuel load was 950l, indicating the prodigious fuel consumption of the *Ferdinand.* Across country the operational range dropped to just 90km.

All in all, the service history of the *Ferdinand/Elefant* does not record one of the German armoured units' greatest achievements, but it should not be forgotten that the vehicle, when it was serviceable, was a potent tank killer.

The story of the *8.8cm Pak 43/3 auf Panzerjäger Panther (Jagdpanther) Sd Kfz 173* is far more positive as it was to become one of the very best of the German *Panzerjäger.* Built onto a *Panther* tank chassis, the relatively spacious fighting compartment that housed the 8.8cm PaK 43/3 was well protected behind sloping armour and the vehicle was fast and highly mobile. Production by MIAG at Braunschweig commenced during December 1943. A second production line was later established at the Maschinenfabrik Niedersachsen – Hannover (MNH) but it did not start production until December 1944 and was bombed out of existence in February 1945. In all 425 units were manufactured, although not all of them were delivered. This total was too limited to have any great effect on the course of the war but wherever the *Jagdpanther* appeared it proved to be difficult

The breech and mounting for an 8.8cm PaK 43/3 in a relatively spacious Jagdpanther *combat compartment.* (P Chamberlain Collection)

to overcome. The 8.8cm PaK 43/3 continued to be supplied by the Dortmund-Hoerder-Hüttenverein Werke at Lippstadt. The first *Jagdpanther* battalion was not fully equipped until June 1944.

Rightly regarded as a redoubtable opponent by the Allies, the *Jagdpanther* saw extensive service on all fronts. It had a combat weight of 46 tonnes and carried a crew of five. Ammunition stowage was provided for up to sixty rounds, although fifty-seven rounds seems to have been a more normal load. Total barrel traverse was 28° and elevation from -8° to +14°. Road speed was a respectable 48km/h and road range was 160km. Close-in defensive fire was supplied by a 7.92mm MG34 machine-gun in a ball mounting on the sloping front hull plate.

One offshoot from the *Jagdpanther* programme was that at one stage during mid- to late 1944 far more PaK 43/3 guns were being manufactured then there were vehicles on which to mount them. Some surplus guns, 418 of them, were therefore assigned to the *Westwall* fortifications where they were meant to be statically emplaced on steel frames set into concrete. As an interim measure some guns were installed on roughly finished timber platforms. The intention was that eventually 450 guns would be so emplaced but by late 1944 and early 1945 parts of the *Westwall* were already being pierced by the advancing Allies. Only a relative few PaK 43/3 guns were installed as planned, and these had little effect.

An American soldier examining an 8.8cm PaK 43/3 gun that was captured while still in the process of being installed as a makeshift anti-tank gun in November 1944. (US National Archives)

The three above-mentioned self-propelled 8.8cm PaK 43 platforms were the only ones to see large-scale service. Their outline details were as follows:

Vehicle	*Nashorn*	*Elefant*	*Jagdpanther*
Crew	4	6	5
Combat weight	24 tonnes	68 tonnes	46 tonnes
Length overall	8,440mm	8,140mm	9,900mm
Height	2,650mm	2,970mm	1,960mm
Width	2,950mm	3,430mm	3,270mm
Max. road speed	40km/h	20km/h	48km/h
Road range	210km	150km	160km
Barrel traverse	30°	28°	28°
Barrel elevation	–5° to +20°	–8° to +14°	–8° to +14°

Kursk

One of the most remarkable things regarding the German *Wehrmacht* during the period when it was at the height of its military powers was its resilience. Just weeks after the German Army had suffered its worst defeat and losses of the war (so far), at Stalingrad during the winter of 1942–1943, it was back on the offensive during February 1943 with a massive drive against Kharkov. Once again the Soviet high command was caught unawares for although they suspected that a German offensive was imminent, they had no firm knowledge of where the blow would fall.

Kharkov duly fell during March along with yet another swathe of Soviet territory – it was the third time the city had changed hands since the start of Operation Barbarossa. One result of the end of the Kharkov fighting was that the line to the north of the city between Soviet and German-held territory was marked by what became known as the Kursk Salient, or Kursk Bulge. This was a massive salient into the German lines, about 200km wide and up to 150km deep, at the centre of which was the important railway and industrial centre of Kursk. Eliminating this bulge was an obvious next move for the Germans, as obvious to the Soviet commanders as it was to their German adversaries. For the first time the Soviet high command had the knowledge of where the next German offensive was to take place.

Eliminating the Kursk Salient would be a great coup for the Germans for inside the bulge was about one-fifth of the Soviet Union's available combat manpower. For what became known as Operation Zitadelle (Operation Citadel) the German General Staff concentrated no less than 50 divisions, 17 of them Panzer or mechanised, and a considerable air fleet numbering 2,109 aircraft. On the ground there would be about 2,700 tanks, 800,000 men and about 10,000 artillery pieces. It was to be the greatest concentration of military power the *Wehrmacht* had yet formed and it had to be, for Operation Zitadelle was to be a considerable undertaking. The intention was to create a 'super-Cannae' where armoured offensives from the north and south of the mouth of the Salient would cut off the forces within the bulge and annihilate them.

The greatest drawback to this plan was that, as mentioned above, it was as obvious a move to the Soviets as it was to the Germans. They were determined that for once they would defeat the German's intentions. Their plans were as straightforward as their opponent's. The German attack would be allowed to enter the Soviet defences only for them to be stopped and ground down before a counter-offensive could be launched to push the Germans back to beyond their start lines. To this end the Soviets made their defensive plans with great care. They intended to defend in depth with at least three defensive lines so arranged that the German advances would have to be made through strong, carefully concealed defensive positions covered by numerous anti-tank minefields, barbed wire, anti-tank ditches dug by civilian labour and lines of artillery covering what would become tank killing grounds. By 1943 the Soviets had developed anti-tank techniques where every available artillery piece, towed and self-propelled, no matter what its calibre or nature, would be turned against any armour that appeared. Field artillery with calibres of 76.2mm became adept at this task for even their high-explosive projectiles could inflict serious damage on almost any

German armoured vehicle. Even the heavy *Tiger* tanks with their 8.8cm KwK 36 main guns proved to be vulnerable when concentrated fire was directed at their relatively thin side armour. In the air fleets of ground-attack aircraft would intervene, while Soviet fighters kept their opposites at bay.

Many German staff officers viewed the forthcoming battle with trepidation and their doubts were increased by Hitler constantly delaying the commencement of operations. He intended to include the new *Panther* tanks in the offensive. Described as the German counter to the T-34 tank series, the untried *Panthers* were only just beginning to come off the production lines and were still largely undeveloped as combat machines. Just 200 were available for the start of the offensive. In addition, Hitler had considerable faith in the abilities of the *Ferdinand*, the heavy *Panzerjäger* created by converting the hulls and running gear of the Porsche *Tiger P* heavy tank that had been developed alongside the Henschel *Tiger*. By the time the Henschel design had been selected in place of the Porsche submission, ninety of the latter chassis had been completed. They therefore had to be used in some manner so they were converted into heavy *Panzerjäger* carrying the 8.8cm PaK 43/2 as their primary armament mounted in a thickly armoured enclosed superstructure added onto the rear of the hull. This rear location for the gun meant that the two petrol engines, driving the generators that in turn provided the power for the final drives, had to be relocated forward inside the hull. These conversions were made in a great hurry, the resultant vehicle remaining under-developed in the rush into service and with many technical shortcomings still to be overcome.

They were formed into two main formations, *schweres Heeres Panzerjäger Abteilung 653 und 654*, each with forty-five vehicles. A total of eighty-nine vehicles actually took part in the initial stages of the attack, divided into about fifteen sub-units to add spear-point punch and fire support to the initial stages of the attack. In effect the *Panzerjäger* were to be deployed as heavy *Sturmgewehr* (assault guns).

Delays with the *Panthers* and the *Ferdinands* therefore inflicted delays on the start of Operation Zitadelle. The original start date was supposed to be 4 May. At first it was put off until 12 June and even that day passed by without the required quantities of *Panthers* and *Ferdinands* in place so the offensive did not begin until 5 July. By then the Soviet high command was more than ready. From all manner of intelligence sources that included spy rings, information from deserters and battlefield surveillance, they had even acquired the time and locations of the initial attacks.

They announced their knowledge by a massive artillery bombardment of the German final assembly areas some 10 minutes before the attack was due to start on 5 July. This disrupted but did not delay the opening attacks, but it did provide the Germans with a nasty foretaste of what was to come. The fortunes of the forty-nine 8.8cm PaK 43/2 armed *Ferdinands* of *schweres Heeres Panzerjäger Abteilung 653*, attacking on a 45km front from the northern tip of the Salient around Zavidovka, were similar to those attacking from the south from Tomarovka. Within hours of the attack moving forward thirty-seven of the forty-nine *Ferdinands* that started were marooned, immobile in anti-tank minefields. Few of these stranded vehicles were as a result of complete knockouts but were mobility kills that blew off tracks and running gear, leaving the rest of the vehicle intact – but motionless and vulnerable. In the haste to get the *Ferdinands* into action no consideration had been given to providing any secondary defensive armament such as machine-guns or other weapon ports. Therefore, they were prone to the attentions of Soviet tank-killer squads that could approach the stranded vehicles undisturbed and wreak their worst against the vehicles' vision devices, remaining running gear and other essentials.

Once immobile, the *Ferdinands* main armament, the 8.8cm PaK 43/2, could do little to provide the anticipated support for the main attack, which soon settled down into prolonged, slogging encounters that slowly, and at great cost, made their way into the maze of Soviet defences. Even so, later analysis revealed that between them the two main *Ferdinand* groups had managed to inflict a reported 120 Soviet tank casualties, plus the destruction of numerous field fortifications. Many of the *Ferdinand* casualties of the first day of operations were later recovered with great difficulty to be repaired and patched up for a return to service, just thirteen from *Abteilung 654* (attacking from the south) being total losses throughout the entire Zitadelle offensive.

Operation Zitadelle ground on for days, culminating in the greatest clash of armour yet seen at the Battle of Prokhovka at the northern tip of the southern thrust. Here on 12 July entire tank armies fought it out under an enormous cloud of dust, while overhead some of the greatest aerial battles of the war were waged, ground-based 8.8cm FlaK 18/36/37 guns playing their part when opportunity arose. By 17 July it became apparent to many in the German high command, apart from a few die-hards, that Operation Zitadelle no longer had any chance of success and the main attacks were called off, especially after Hitler felt it necessary to divert some of his Panzer assets to Sicily where the Allies had just made an amphibious landing. Operations around the Salient continued for another month even as the planned Soviet counter-offensive began in earnest.

Throughout it all the *Ferdinands*, by then acting as a mobile defensive reserve, were rushed hither and thither to break up Soviet tank thrusts, knock out field fortifications and even take part in individual battles. One report mentions a Soviet T-34 being knocked out by a *Ferdinand* with a single shot from a range of over 4,700m, so the *Ferdinands* were able to display their tank-killing potential on more than one occasion. In fact by the time the aftermath of Operation Zitadelle had reached a final halt at the end of August 1943 it was calculated that they had managed to knock out at least 500 Soviet tanks at a cost of 44 of their own number destroyed.

By the end of August the Soviet counter-offensive was still in full swing, driving back the Germans to the extent that Kharkov changed hands yet again, this time for good. The German super-Cannae never occurred, the German losses being prodigious and increasingly difficult to replace. The Soviets lost even more in terms of men and materiel but they made one important gain – they had won the strategic initiative. Until Kursk the Germans had always held that initiative. They could strike as and when they thought fit. After Kursk they were always on the defensive (apart from a few local initiatives) and from then on they began to fall back towards the West instead of advancing towards the East. Time was to show that the Battle of the Kursk Salient was the major turning point of the Second World War, a battle in which 88s once again played their part.

This vehicle was the prototype produced by Krupp and Steyr to act as the Waffentrager *for an 8.8cm PaK 43/3.* (P Chamberlain Collection)

The next three vehicles in the check-list were all 1944–1945 prototype vehicles based on the Czech PzKpfw 38(t) light tank chassis. By 1944 this well-tried basic chassis had been developed by the Germans into many forms that its original pre-1938 designers would not have recognised. Gradually the hull became wider, the drive train became increasingly dependable and the chassis also proved to be highly adaptable. As carriers of the 8.8cm PaK 43/3, the three prototypes all carried the main gun in open 360° traverse mountings and were intended not so much as *Panzerjäger* but as *leichte Waffentrager*, or light weapon carriers. As such

Another prototype, this design foray was proposed by Ardelt as a Waffentrager *to carry an 8.8cm PaK 43/3.* (P Chamberlain Collection)

An alternative view of the Ardelt Waffentrager *carrying an 8.8cm PaK 43/3*. (TJ Gander Collection)

they were intended to carry and perhaps emplace weapons around a battlefield rather than act as combat vehicles. None of the three prototypes was considered suitable for service, although some of them saw limited action during the latter stages of the war. More design work on further vehicles along the same lines was planned by Ardelt in conjunction with Krupp. All the three vehicles actually completed weighed between 15 and 15.5 tonnes. As *leichte Waffentrager* there were plans developed for these vehicles, or vehicles similar to them, to carry an array of weapons, including an adapted 8.8cm KwK 43, some of them with very light armoured protection.

Relating to the last item in the above check-list, the 8.8cm PaK 43/3 was reportedly mounted on only a few of the 70-tonne *Jagdtiger* monsters, and then only as an expedient measure after Allied bombing raids disrupted production of the vehicle's intended main armament, the 12.8cm PaK 44 or 80.

One further projected carrier for the 8.8cm PaK 43/3 was a self-propelled mounting on a *PzKpfw IV* tank chassis designated the Wg IV. The gun was positioned towards the rear in a manner similar to, but lower, than on the *Nashorn*. The intention was that the barrel could traverse 30° and elevate from -4° to +14°. The project did not leave the drawing board, probably because the design offered few advantages over the existing *Nashorn*.

There remains one odd offshoot of associations between the 8.8cm PaK 43 series and self-propelled mountings. This idea originated during 1943 when it was decided to investigate the possibilities of developing an armoured-vehicle gun mounting that would not require a recoil system. The intention was that all recoil forces would be absorbed by the mass of the carrier vehicle, the gun being rigidly mounted directly onto hull armour or chassis members. One main objective of this proposal was to reduce the number of man hours and raw materials needed for production. Other potential advantages included reduced in-service maintenance requirements, and making more space available within the host vehicles.

The early exploratory work was carried out under the direction of a Professor Waninger, who supervised research work by Alkett and, later, Rheinmetall. Early experiments were carried out using a captured Soviet 120mm mortar secured to a *Wespe* chassis that normally combined a *PzKpfw II* light-tank hull and running gear with a 105mm howitzer. This was only a feasibility study as trials continued with a 7.5cm PaK 39 rigidly mounted on a *Panzerjäger 38(t) Hetzer*, the tank-killer derivative of the Czech *PzKpfw 38(t)* light tank. By that stage the rigid mounting had acquired the name of *Starr* (literally, inflexible or stiff). Gradual development moved the gun to a central position on the sloping front plate of the hull and the original gimbal mounting was replaced by a Rheinmetall-designed ball mounting. In addition, alterations were introduced to the gun control linkages. About ten *Hetzers* with the *Starr* mounting were just entering the pre-production stage when the war ended – none reached the troops.

The seeming success of the *Starr Hetzer* prompted Krupp technicians to experiment with a similar mounting for the 8.8cm PaK 43/3 on a *Jagdpanther*. They proposed that the gun would have to be mounted further to the rear than usual and that the gun's rear seating could be kept constant by a powerful spring. The elevating brackets were to have been mounted on the superstructure floor plate. Development work was still in progress with this mounting when the end of the war terminated any further progress.

It is noticeable that since 1945 further investigations into rigidly mounted combat-vehicle guns have been conspicuous by their absence. Doubtless it was at least partially influenced by the fact that of the few examples of the *Starr Hetzer* that survived after the war to be adopted by the new Czecho-Slovak army, all were subsequently converted to accept conventional recoil mountings.

The Soviet 88s

The opening phases of Operation Barbarossa, the German invasion of the Soviet Union in June 1941, brought a large quantity of captured war materiel into the German armoury. More materiel was to follow as the invasion swept deeper into the Soviet Union. Included in the vast haul were the three standard Soviet heavy anti-aircraft guns, the 76.2mm Model 1931, the 76.2mm Model 1938 and the 85mm Model 1939. All three of these models were robust, straightforward designs

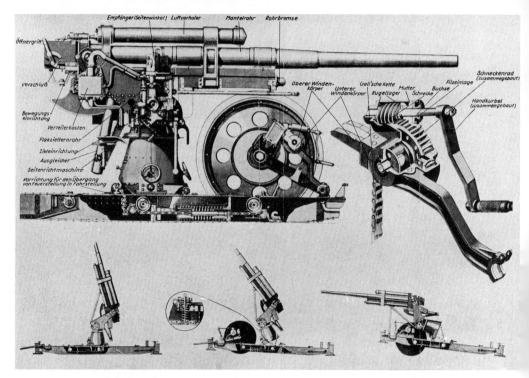

A page from a German manual relating to the 7.62/8.8cm FlaK M 31(r). (TJ Gander Collection)

An example of a 76.2mm Model 1931 surviving in Finland. Only a few of these types of gun were bored out to accommodate 88mm ammunition but those that were so processed remained much the same externally. (TJ Gander)

This photograph of a Soviet 85mm Model 1939 was taken at the Museum of Artillery in St Petersburg. Those rebored to 88mm calibre by the Germans remained externally identical.
(TJ Gander)

mounted on highly mobile carriages, two of them generally similar to that of the German 88 but far simpler overall, especially in relation to the wheeled carriage units.

The 76.2mm Model 1931 was based on an imported Swedish Bofors design, having remote affinities to the German 88. During the development of the Soviet gun some modifications were introduced by Rheinmetall technicians assisting their Soviet counterparts at the Red Putilov Factory, Leningrad (now St Petersburg). In its original form the gun and carriage were carried on a single-axle travelling carriage, but by 1939 this was being replaced by a twin-axle unit, originally developed for the replacement gun for the Model 1931, the 76.2mm Model 1938. This twin-axle arrangement was again based on a Swedish Bofors design. The 76.2mm Model 1938 introduced some further improvements over the Model 1931, including a revised, heavier barrel.

From 1939 onwards these two guns were supplemented by the 85mm Model 1939 (52-K or KS-12), later rated as the best Soviet anti-aircraft gun fielded during the Great Patriotic War. It carried over the twin-axle travelling carriage of the 76.2mm Model 1938 and was recognisable by the presence of a muzzle brake. In most other respects these two guns were similar, other than in their calibres. The overall performance of the 85mm Model 1939 was similar to that of the German 88s but it was not often deployed by the Soviets in the direct-fire ground role – they preferred to retain them for the air defence of rear areas.

So many of these Soviet anti-aircraft guns were captured that any undamaged examples were taken into the German inventory. Few were issued to *Luftwaffe* FlaK batteries as most went to various local home-defence militias, recruited from factory workers, or to the *Hitler-Jugend*. In both instances they acted more as local morale boosters than as auxiliary air-defence units. In addition to these guns, seventy-two of the 85mm Model 1939 guns were sent to Norway, where they were incorporated into the local air and coastal defences. When all these captured guns were first issued they continued to fire stocks of captured Soviet ammunition.

When captured stocks began to run low a decision was made in 1943 to re-bore the barrels to accept standard German 8.8cm FlaK 18/36/37 ammunition, the actual re-boring operations being carried out at German-controlled factories in Northern Italy. The measure was intended to simplify logistics and prolong the service life of the captured guns. Few of the 76.2mm Model 1931 guns (known to the Germans as the 7.62cm FlaK 31(r)) underwent the re-boring process as it was considered that the barrels were too lightly constructed; those few became the 7.62/8.8cm FlaK M 31(r). Many of the Model 1931 guns had been scrapped by 1944 but during that year seventy-two, still in their 76.2mm calibre, were passed to Finland by Germany, where they were renovated and added to the forty-seven guns already captured from the Soviets by the Finns themselves.

The other two gun models were re-bored and re-issued to the auxiliary air defence and Norwegian batteries in some numbers – at least 192 barrels were involved. New designations were allotted. The 76.2mm Model 1938 became the 7.62/8.8cm FlaK M 38(r), while the 85mm Model 1939 became the 8.5/8.8cm FlaK M 39(r). In this form both guns served on in Germany until the war ended. The 72 FlaK M 39(r) guns based in Norway were also provided with 88mm barrels and later served on as coastal-defence guns as part of the Norwegian coast-defence forces until 1962.

Basic outline data for these guns was as follows:

	FlaK M 31(r)	FlaK M 38(r)	FlaK M 39(r)
Original calibre	76.2mm	76.2mm	85mm
Re-bored calibre	88mm	88mm	88mm
Length (calibres)	55	55	55.2
Length of barrel	4,191mm	4,191mm	4,693mm
Weight of barrel	830kg	920kg	920kg
Weight complete	4,820kg	4,210kg	4,220kg
Weight emplaced	3,650kg	3,047kg	3,057kg
Length overall	6,700mm	5,150mm	5,150mm
Width travelling	1,300mm	2,250mm	2,250mm
Width emplaced	2,210mm	4,800mm	4,800mm
Height	2,320mm	2,220mm	2,220mm
Traverse	360°	360°	360°
Elevation	–2° to +82°	–3° to + 82°	–2° to +82°
Crew	11	11	11

Naval 88s

There remains one further series of 88mm gun to be mentioned, but these bear no relationship to any of the 88mm guns mentioned so far (other than a distant relationship to the Rheinmetall 88mm anti-aircraft gun of the First World War). They were naval guns with origins dating back to the period of rapid German naval expansion that occurred during the first decade of the twentieth century.

The guns involved all belonged to a category that can be named as the 8.8cm SK series, with the SK denoting *Schiffs Kanone*, or naval gun. The only point of similarity between these naval guns and the 88mm guns described so far here were the calibre, plus the fact that one of the naval projectiles developed for them was used as the basis of the Illuminating projectile fired from the FlaK 18/36/37 series. Generally speaking, the naval 88mm guns were passable performers compared to their *Luftwaffe* and *Heer* counterparts. They were sound, well-tested guns produced in several forms and on a bewildering variety of mountings, both for firing at surface targets and for air-defence purposes – some mountings managed to combine both roles.

Few of the original, pre-First World War 8.8cm SK had survived by the 1930s, other than as training weapons at naval establishments (nearly all 8.8cm SK having gone down with their ships when they were scuttled at Scapa Flow). By the end of the 1930s no fewer than four updated models had been issued

The Rheinmetall 8.8cm SK C/35, a naval gun that had nothing in common with the other 88mm guns described in this book other than sharing the same 88mm calibre. (TJ Gander)

to the *Kriegsmarine*, the SK C/30, SK C/31, SK C/32 and SK C/35, the C/ denoting *Construktion* or model, together with the year of acceptance for service. All were designed and manufactured by Rheinmetall at Düsseldorf and so were their mountings.

Of the examples quoted, the SK C/31and SK C/32 were dedicated, high-performance anti-aircraft guns with 72-calibre barrels having a maximum effective ceiling of 13,300m. Only a few were completed, usually on twin-barrel mountings, as the *Kriegsmarine* came to favour the 105mm calibre for the air defence of their capital ships.

The other two guns were multi-functional 45-calibre guns with variations between them such as differing chamber capacities and performances to match. The SK C/30 had a horizontal sliding block and a muzzle brake. The SK C/35 had a vertical sliding block and lacked a muzzle brake. As already mentioned, the mountings could vary widely, the most unusual perhaps being the *Unterseeboot Lafette C/35*, developed specifically for the 8.8cm SK C/35 guns carried by Type VII U-boats and thus able to withstand prolonged immersion in salt water. Some mountings had gun shields, others did not. Ammunition types included high explosive (with or without tracer), high-explosive incendiary, armour piercing and Illuminating.

As early as 1940 the planned German naval construction programme was already being cut back to concentrate on land and aviation manufacturing priorities. That left numerous completed naval guns without a naval role to fulfil, among them being the 8.8cm SK series. The *Kriegsmarine* deployed some of these surplus guns to arm minesweepers and similar light vessels (including the convoy escort *Artillerieträger* based on barges), as well as to defend their harbours and dockyards, but eventually the demands of Hitler's *Atlantikwall* meant that many non-essential naval guns had to be diverted to coast defence, and that is where many of the 8.8cm SK series guns ended up.

Outline details of just one of these guns, the multi-function 8.8cm SK C/35, (and probably the most numerous by 1945), are provided to 'complete' the 88 picture:

DATA FOR SK C/35	
Calibre	88mm
Length of piece	3,985mm (L/45.28)
Length of barrel	3,731mm (L/42.4)
Length of rifling	3,3135mm
Weight of gun and breech	776kg
Weight emplaced	*c.* 2,425kg
Traverse	360°
Elevation	–10° to +30°
Chamber capacity	2,490cc
Muzzle velocity	AP and HE, 700m/s; Illuminating, 600m/s
Projectile weight	AP and HE, 9kg; Illuminating, 9.04kg
Propellant weight	2.1kg
Rate of fire	15 to 20rds/min
Max. range	11,950m at +30°
Service life	approx. 12,000 efc

Chapter 5

Operations

Although the 88 gained its awesome reputation as an anti-tank gun it should never be forgotten that its origins were as an anti-aircraft gun. It was as an anti-aircraft gun that the 88s bore the brunt of Germany's air defences, one indication of its importance being that of the 13,260 heavy anti-aircraft guns defending the *Reich* in August 1944, 10,930 were 88s of one model or another. By that date the FlaK 18/36/37 series was approaching obsolescence as their bomber targets began to fly higher and faster than ever, but the stalwarts soldiered on and were still coming off the production lines as the war ended.

A battery of 8.8cm FlaK 18s firing at what appears to be a training range. The equipment in the foreground in a Kommandogerat *controlling the four visible guns.* (P Chamberlain Collection)

Night firing by an 8.8cm FlaK 36 by one of the six six-gun 88 batteries based on Guernsey in the Channel Islands. (CIOS Guernsey Archives)

In general terms the air defence of the home *Reich* was purely a *Luftwaffe* responsibility, although the policy development of the FlaK arm had been the remit of the *Heereswaffenamt* (the staff bureau dealing with equipment supply and development matters (HWA), mainly an Army orientated organisation) since 1927. While the HWA was responsible for the development and production of all Army weapons, three branches were involved in the development of anti-aircraft guns. These comprised *Waffen Prüfung 1* (Wa Prüf 1 – Weapon Trials 1) which dealt with ammunition matters, Wa Prüf 3 which dealt with ballistics, and Wa Prüf 10 which concerned itself with the guns themselves. By 1939 the *Luftwaffe* had gained a significant foothold in this organisation so that by 1939 the anti-aircraft aspects of Wa Prüf 1, 3 and 10 had been largely taken over by the German Air Ministry to become the *General Luftzeugmeister, Amtsgruppe für FlaK Entwicklung*, usually abbreviated to *GL FlaK E* (Air Force Equipment Branch, FlaK Development Section). However, HWA and its *Waffen Prüfung* branches still retained a place in the development and testing of new FlaK weapons and part of the responsibility for placing production contracts.

Over the years the *Luftwaffe* built up a complex and efficient early warning and signals network that covered the entire country to alert the nation of approaching enemy aircraft and control their defence resources once they arrived over German territory. Every city and industrial centre acquired its local gun defences, all controlled by a vast communication web that became one of the most cohesive and longest lasting of the German command systems.

This network took time to create for it was originally established to serve as a very modest defensive measure. In the absence of any meaningful experience with which to work, its original form was based on training school data where the number of rounds fired to damage an airborne target was transposed into operational calculations relating to the strengths of gun defences needed. At one stage during the early 1930s it became an accepted dictum that an airborne target would be hit for every forty-seven rounds fired. What this transposition overlooked was that at the training schools the gun crews fired only at (often unrealistic) targets they thought they could hit, a situation that could not be carried over to operational circumstances. It was also failed to take into account that back in 1918, when the Army controlled the air-defence guns, 5,040 rounds had to be fired between hits on an enemy aircraft. Post-1939 experience was to demonstrate that those 1918 results were to be exceeded by a wide margin in ammunition expenditure terms.

Thus in 1939 the Western border of Germany was defended by a thin belt of 197 gun positions, some of them having just one gun that was supposed to defend a wide area of territory. Once the air war started in earnest that situation soon changed, the minimum number of guns allocated to a single position or battery being at least four and eventually six. Demands for more and more guns flowed into the supply chain at a time when every sector of the *Wehrmacht* was calling for more and more air-defence guns and their associated equipments. With these demands came a major reorganisation of the *Luftwaffe* air-defence arm, which was soon put to the test.

The largest of the *Luftwaffe* anti-aircraft units emerged as the *FlaKdivision*, the formal establishment of which is outlined below. However, it must be stressed that few, if any, of the *FlaKdivision* were fortunate enough to field such an array of personnel and equipment. Personnel totals were frequently under strength, their numbers being swelled by reservists, auxiliary militias such as the *ReichsArbeiterDienst* (RAD) workers' militias, females in uniform operating switchboards or searchlights and even *Hitler-Jugend* 'helpers' (*Luftwaffenhelfer*). Equipment of all kinds was usually at a premium so equipment totals were often topped up by the incorporation of captured or ancient substitutes.

	Div HQ	Sig Bn	S'light Regt	Gun Regt	Gun Regt	Gun Regt	Med
Personnel	200	300	2,043	2,448	2,448	2,448	250
LMG	2	11	29	38	38	38	22
2cm FlaK	–	–	–	52	52	52	–
2cm FlaKV	–	–	–	9	9	9	–
3.7cm FlaK	–	–	–	12	12	12	–
8.8cm FlaK	–	–	–	24	24	24	–
10.5cm FlaK	–	–	–	16	16	16	–
60cm S'light	–	–	–	16	16	16	–
105cm S'light	–	–	90	–	–	–	–
200cm S'light	–	–	18	–	–	–	–
Balloons	–	–	–	72	72	72	–
Vehicles	30	44	94	109	109	109	37
Trailers	1	12	255	238	238	238	–
Motor cycles	20	10	52	55	55	55	2

From the above it can be seen that a *FlaKdivision* was a sizeable military organisation but, it has to be stressed, it is highly unlikely that a fully equipped and populated formation at the strengths shown ever existed.

The *EisenbahnFlaK* units also came under the control of the *Luftwaffe*. They were grouped in regiments, each composed of three heavy battalions or two heavy and one light battalion. Each battalion had three or four batteries, usually with one battery to a train.

Each 88mm gun had the potential to bring down an Allied heavy bomber with one round but getting that round to the correct place at the correct time was no easy matter. There was also the unfortunate realisation that 88mm high-explosive projectiles were not as efficient as had been expected against modern aircraft. The standard high-explosive projectiles relied on their body fragmentation to inflict the necessary damage and to achieve this called for a 'near-miss' detonation occurring less than 30m from the target aircraft (a detonation had to occur less than 9m from a target to be fairly certain of bringing an aircraft down), the instant of high-explosive payload ignition being controlled by the projectile's time fuse. Not until the last year of the war was a percussion element added to the time futes and then only after experiments demonstrated that a single 88mm projectile containing an explosive payload weighing as little as 400g could bring down a four-engined heavy bomber – if it actually hit the aircraft.

At the control level, the deployment of anti-aircraft guns to defend the *Reich* was an ever-changing scene to meet an ever-increasing threat. When the Allied bomber fleets started to grow in numbers and range, to say nothing of all-round improvements in performance and weapon-carrying capability, many FlaK guns were withdrawn from field units to assume home-defence duties. This change was reflected in the growing manufacturing practice of producing /2 guns and mountings for static concrete emplacements only, so increasing numbers were delivered without cruciform firing platforms, wheeled carriages or tractors. While this practice saved considerable manufacturing potential that could be diverted to other priorities, it still entailed a considerable alternative outlay in concrete, manpower, accommodation and transport resources.

Another shortcoming in the gradual change to concrete emplacements came when Allied bombers started to concentrate and prolong their efforts against major targets, such as Hamburg or the Ruhr, and introduced the thousand-bomber raids. These changing tactics usually overwhelmed the local defences, while other guns statically emplaced nearby were unable to do anything useful in defensive terms as there was no way they could be moved to the afflicted areas in time. As mentioned elsewhere, one partial counter to this situation was the formation of *EisenbahnFlaK* railway batteries but even these could contribute little by late 1944, a time when Allied air superiority made rail travel a hazardous activity. Also by late 1944, ever-increasing numbers of static anti-aircraft gun

A standard text-book illustration of an 8.8cm FlaK 18 in action with all visible personnel in their drill-book positions. (P Chamberlain Collection)

An 8.8cm FlaK 36/2 or FlaK 37/2 installed in a full fortress standard installation. The personnel in the foreground are opening the armoured door to one of the ready-use magazine compartments. (P Chamberlain Collection)

positions were being overrun by the advancing Allied land forces and their precious guns were being lost in ever-increasing numbers.

But the air defences of the *Reich* did have their successes. As many as 2,500 Allied aircraft were brought down during July 1943 (not all of them by gun fire) but that freak high was never repeated. Some of those massive casualty totals were as a result of the implementation of new defensive measures such as the introduction of radar to fire-control procedures, improved night-fighter techniques and the advent of the *Gross-Batterie*. The latter involved combinations of up to three FlaK batteries all firing on one designated target rather than each battery selecting its own. Visible selected targets were tracked by the three *Kommandogeräte* assigned to the three batteries involved so that the fire of all three batteries could thus be readily concentrated, the survival chances of the unfortunate selected target being thereby much reduced. At night a single *Würzburg* radar was employed to control all three batteries.

The results of the *Gross-Batterie* approach were very encouraging until a misguided high-level decision was made to enlarge the system to combine no less than twenty-four guns firing as a single battery, all under the control of a single *Kommandogerät*. This approach produced the *Mammoth-Batterie*, which, for various technical reasons, was a much less viable proposition in terms of inflicting aircraft casualties. But once the decision was made it was stubbornly adhered to so the true potential of the *Gross-Batterie* was never fully realised.

Gun crews running to their positions to fend off an Allied air attack within range of an 8.8cm FlaK 18 battery somewhere on the coast of Greece. (P Chamberlain Collection)

Once outside Germany and in the various occupied territories the anti-aircraft command structure was rather more fragmented as the *Luftwaffe* batteries were gradually supplemented by Army batteries. The Army anti-aircraft organisation differed slightly from that of the *Luftwaffe*, this being one result of Army field formations relying on the *Luftwaffe* for heavy anti-aircraft defence up until about 1941, after which time the Army (and *Waffen SS*) began to acquire heavy anti-aircraft 88mm guns of their own. Until then Army air defences consisted of 20mm and 37mm FlaK weapons only.

The Army's basic division-level anti-aircraft formation was the regiment and they could be of two types, motorised or non-motorised. Within each type of regiment the two- or three-gun-equipped battalions could be either heavy or mixed. Both types of battalion contained 20mm and 88mm guns but in the heavy battalions the emphasis was on 88mm weapons, with only a relatively few 20mm guns.

The composition of a non-motorised, heavy anti-aircraft battalion, the type most likely to be allocated to garrison and occupation formations, was as follows:

	Bn HQ	Com Sec	Bty	Bty	Bty	Bty
Personnel	76	19	104	104	104	104
LMG	1	2	2	2	2	2
2cm FlaK	–	–	2	2	2	2
8.8cm FlaK	–	–	6	6	6	6
Vehicles	15	4	2	2	2	2
Trailers	7	–	9	9	9	9
Motor cycles	3	1	2	2	2	2

As elsewhere, these formal establishments could vary widely in both personnel and equipment terms. Purely static air-defence units would contain fewer personnel, and Army 88mm strengths could vary according to the type of division to which they were allotted. An indication of this can be seen from the following:

Formation	Number of 88mm guns
Infantry Division	12
Motorised Division	8
Panzer Division	8
SS Panzer Division	12
Luftwaffe Parachute Division	12

Many Army divisions never did acquire their own heavy anti-aircraft gun assets and had to continue to rely on their usual allocation of 2cm and 3.7cm light FlaK guns.

The relaxed crew of an 8.8cm FlaK 36 during what appears to be an easy going gun-drill training session. (P Chamberlain Collection)

A K3 loading a round into the breech of an 8.8cm FlaK 36. The timber housing over the recoil cylinder was a weather-protection measure often employed when guns were installed in permanent or semi-permanent positions. (CIOS Guernsey Archives)

Each 88mm gun had a crew of up to eleven, although on a purely static battery the number of gunners actually manning a gun could be as few as six. Of the eleven gunners allotted to each gun, one was the towing vehicle driver and another the detachment commander. When serving the gun in action their duties were as follows, the K standing for *Kanonier* or gunner:

K1	Layer for elevation
K2	Layer for line (traverse)
K3	Loader
K4	Ammunition handler
K5	Ammunition handler

K6	Fuse-setting machine operator
K7	Fuse setter (machine loader)
K8	Ammunition handler
K9	Ammunition handler.

On the FlaK 41 an extra gunner assisted in elevation control. Captured Soviet anti-aircraft guns also had a full crew of eleven.

Anti-tank

For all its many successes the 8.8cm FlaK 18 and 36 were not suited to the anti-tank role for four main reasons: the guns were high, bulky, heavy and difficult to hide. For ideal protection each gun required a great deal of effort to dig in and conceal as when pressed into action in the open the gun crews were highly vulnerable to in-coming small arms and artillery fire. Even the addition of a shield (some with hinged sides) could not protect the crew from artillery air bursts. The crews therefore had to become experts in getting their guns in and out of action in a minimum of time. In this they were helped by the introduction of the *Sonderanhänger 202*, which meant that the gun muzzle pointed away from the towing vehicle, towards the rear and facing the enemy.

Another problem encountered when attempting to utilise the 88 as an anti-armour weapon was that, in the normal course of events, the guns were unlikely to be anywhere near where they were needed. The normal location of any heavy anti-aircraft gun supporting field units would have been in rear areas to defend combat support and supply facilities rather than covering a combat area. If an 88 was to be deployed in the anti-armour role it made sense to select carefully and prepare a firing position well before action commenced, rather than rush to a position when an enemy threat developed. Many of the most emphatic 88 successes were from pre-selected ambush positions. The drawback to this pre-preparation was that once emplaced as anti-tank weapons the guns involved could not be available to fulfil their prime function of air defence. However, it was particularly noticeable on the Eastern Front that more 88s were employed as anti-armour weapons than for air defence.

Other shortcomings of the 88 in the anti-armour role included the fact that the gun itself was far from user-friendly. Designed for an anti-aircraft gun that was meant to be loaded with the barrel in an elevated position, the breech was high and awkward to load with the barrel in the horizontal position, the physical effort necessary to repeatedly raise and load a round weighing up to about 15kg to almost head height being considerable. The aimer was not well served either, for little thought had been given to the direct-fire role at the design stage so his position was awkward and far from comfortable. Perhaps the most unwieldy

The crew of an 8.8cm FlaK 18 await the approach of Allied ground targets from behind a sandbag sangar. (P Chamberlain Collection)

aspect of the gun was its all-round weight which made even limited handling tedious and strenuous for the crew.

The 88 had to be forced into the anti-armour role for the first time in 1940, when the Germans discovered the hard way that Allied tanks such as the British Matildas and the French Char B1 had armoured protection that the then-standard

A hastily emplaced 88 in action on the Eastern Front. (P Chamberlain Collection)

An 88 firing at a ground target somewhere in North Africa. One of the crew by the bogie is operating a hand-held rangefinder. (P Chamberlain Collection)

German anti-tank guns could not defeat. In 1940 the little 3.7cm PaK 35/36 proved to be inadequate against all but the lightest of the British and French armoured vehicles, while the larger calibre field artillery pieces lacked suitable armour-piercing ammunition. The pressing of 88s into the anti-armour role was, in 1940, very much a field improvisation, but the lesson was learned that the Germans had a potent anti-tank asset to eke out their anti-armour inventory until

A unconventionally camouflaged 8.8cm FlaK 36 in position on the Lake Ilmen front, Russia, March 1943. (TJ Gander Collection)

An 88 in action somewhere in North Africa. (P Chamberlain Collection)

something better suited to the task could be developed and supplied. In addition, the 88 proved to be very useful against field fortifications and concrete bunkers.

It was in the North African deserts that the 88s came into their own. The generally flat and open terrain enabled the 88s to take full advantage of their prime combat asset, namely range. British tanks encountering emplaced 88s were frequently fired on at ranges far beyond those from which they could retaliate, while at ranges of 2,000m or more the relatively light-armoured protection of

Street fighting involving an 88 in an Italian city, believed to be Florence (Firenze). (P Chamberlain Collection)

most of the Allied tanks then fielded could be penetrated. As an extra morale depressant the first intimation (and last) that an Allied tank crew often had of an encounter with an 88 was a high-velocity, base-fused, armour-piercing projectile exploding inside their vehicle.

Eventually the British Eighth Army abandoned their 'cavalry charge' tank-attack tactics and learned to be wary of German feints that drew their tanks on to carefully emplaced 88s. By then the German 88s were reaping a new crop of unsuspecting tanks in the Soviet Union and were later to gather a fresh harvest against the inexperienced (and over-confident) American armoured units that tried to defeat the Germans during the early battles of the 1942–1943 Tunisian campaign.

As well as being employed in the anti-armour role, the FlaK 18 and 36 were also deployed as indirect-fire field pieces on occasion. While this was rather a waste of their potential, their range was often useful to reach deep into assembly and supply areas with time-fused high-explosive projectiles. When this role was undertaken the fuse setter abandoned his machine and set the time fuses by hand with a setting key. The layer had a rather unenviable task as the dial sight involved in indirect artillery fire was mounted in a clamp on top of the recuperator cylinder. To gain access to the sight the layer had to clamber up and over the gun and expose himself to any counter-artillery fire that may have been directed against their position. The sight was also used to align the gun with the battery's fire-control *Kommandogerät* once the guns had arrived at a new air-defence fire position.

After late 1943 the introduction of the 8.8cm PaK 43/41 and PaK 43 largely overcame the difficulties encountered by the earlier FlaK-based guns. Lower, well protected and relatively easy to conceal, as well as possessing a higher all-round ballistic performance, the new guns proved to be a great and immediate success, even if the bulk and weight of the ungainly PaK 43/41 was a disadvantage on occasion. Their one weakness was that, as far as the German ground forces were concerned, there were never enough of them.

The dedicated 88mm anti-tank guns were usually allocated to *FestungsPaK Kompanies* as part of a *FestungsPaK Battalion*, of which there were several in any Army Sector under the control of a local *FestungsPaK Verband*. This latter unit answered direct to the local Army Command.

Operation Goodwood

Contrary to accepted military wisdom, and too many precedents, the amphibious landings that formed the main part of Operation Overlord, the Allied invasion of Normandy on 6 June 1944, went more or less according to plan. Once a bridgehead had been gained a general lack of German preparedness, plus Allied subterfuges that the main invasion was to take place later in the Pas de Calais, meant that the main German riposte could not take place until some time after the Allies were firmly ashore and in sufficient numbers to meet any German retaliation. It was not long before the Allies had gained a superiority in virtually everything that mattered: in the air; in weapon numbers; and in combat soldiers on the ground.

Throughout June 1944 the Allied bridgehead gradually expanded but not on the scale that was needed. Space within the bridgehead, which stretched from the Contentin Peninsula in the west to east of Caen, came to be at a premium. More and more space was needed for airstrips, ammunition and supply dumps, vehicle parks, field workshops, medical facilities, command centres and all the many other necessaries of modern warfare. As the month progressed, German resistance to outward expansion stiffened noticeably to the point that on many sectors advances were forced to a halt.

This was particularly discernible on the extreme left of the Allied bridgehead around Caen. Behind Caen was wide open country eminently suitable for the airstrips needed by the increasingly effective strike fighter squadrons, which pinned down German movements during daylight hours. The problem was that the Germans still held Caen and fiercely resisted all attempts to take it. In the end the ancient city was simply bombed into rubble by 450 aircraft of Bomber Command, 6 of which were shot down by the ever-present 88s defending the city. The Germans withdrew from the ruins only to take up defensive positions just beyond the outskirts of what had become a heap of rubble, and from there they thwarted several Allied (mainly British and Canadian) attempts to advance further.

Gradually the Allied forces moved forward at great cost until the time was deemed suitable for a breakthrough and Operation Goodwood was born. The plan was for a massed British armoured thrust to be made to the east of Caen, to advance across the German front to take the all-important and commanding Bourgébus Ridge with a view to breaking through with the ultimate intention of taking Falaise, a town some 32km inland. Another objective, mentioned more after the battle than before, was to draw German reserves to the eastern end of the bridgehead to make the planned American breakout in the west more feasible.

Operations commenced on the morning of 18 July. For starters the advanced German positions suffered what was one of the biggest airborne bombing raids on any battlefield yet staged. The damage inflicted by the three massed waves of British and American heavy bombers was tremendous, tanks as large as *Tigers* being overturned by the blast and positions destroyed. Artillery and heavy naval guns joined in. But, as ever, enough Germans survived the bombing and shelling and soon recovered to fight on, and fight on they did.

The defenders were aided by several shortcomings in the Allied plans. The main thrust east of Caen had to cross the water obstacle of the Canal du Caen but this meant that the main force of 1st British Corps had to cross using just six small bridges. It was not long before massive traffic jams formed to hinder progress. Once across another shortcoming arose – the presence of large minefields, some of them laid by the British themselves before the scope of Operation Goodwood was realised. These minefields further delayed and channelled forward movements by the armour. In addition to all this, the Allies had little intelligence of what forces the Germans had or exactly where they were. They were soon to find out the hard way. This was compounded by the fact that, due to their numerous excellent observation points on the ridges overlooking the landscape around Caen, the German high command knew exactly what was to happen and when, and had prepared accordingly.

The traffic confusion at the canal crossings and past the minefields meant that delays accumulated until a fateful decision was made. It was planned to press ahead with just the tanks, leaving behind the mutually supporting infantry, combat-engineer and other units that had previously been found necessary for successful armoured operations. Even the artillery was left behind, and to make things worse the forward controller vehicle needed to guide supporting strike aircraft was soon knocked out so little organised air support was available for the advancing armour.

The tanks, many with crews going into action for the first time, made their way towards the Bourgébus Ridge, almost all the while fighting against German tanks (including *Tigers*) as they progressed. The area below the Ridge was wide open country thought 'suitable for tanks' but, as events were to demonstrate, the terrain was equally suitable for artillery defence. Along the Ridge the Germans had emplaced an unbroken line of artillery positions of all kinds, among them the 88s. Only a relative handful of these were the latest 8.8cm PaK models, most of them being the well-tried 8.8cm FlaK 18/36/37 in carefully prepared emplacements. 21 Panzer Division alone were able to field seventy-eight 88s, this number being swelled, sometimes reluctantly in view of Allied aircraft activities, by the 88s of the 16 *Luftwaffe* Field Division. Just four of the latter's guns that had somehow survived the earlier bombing were responsible for knocking out twelve British tanks near Cagny. A single 88 commanding the Caen–Vimont railway line was responsible for knocking out another twelve tanks.

The massed artillery brought the British armour to a definite halt by knocking out tank after tank, littering the landscape with columns of smoke. The vast bulk of the British armour within 1st British Corps was either Cromwells or American M4 Shermans. Both were inadequately armoured to withstand fire of the weight that descended upon them, the M4 being particularly vulnerable to the extent that, due to the internal layout of their ammunition and fuel storage, a single hit from an 88 was usually sufficient to set them ablaze – the M4 Sherman gained the unfortunate nickname of 'Tommy Cooker'. Throughout the attack on the Bourgébus Ridge the armour was devoid of any form of support, not even artillery. Artillery might have been able to suppress some of the deadly fire that descended on the vehicles but was unable to demonstrate this for the simple reason that the artillery was unable to advance to within range of the Ridge. What limited fire could be supplied was delivered at extreme range.

A column of Cromwell tanks passing a captured 8.8cm PaK 43/41 during the Operation Goodwood fighting. (P Chamberlain Collection)

Fighting around the Caen perimeter continued in deteriorating weather until 20 July, but the final territorial results remained much the same as they were on the evening of 18 July.

Due in part to the 88, Operation Goodwood failed at the cost of over 5,500 soldiers and 400 tanks. The lost tanks were easy to replace. Thanks to American industry the Allies had so many at their disposal that they were replaced within days. Replacing the soldiers was not so easy.

War year users

During the Second World War 88s served with several user nations other than Germany. Between 1936 and 1945 it was felt necessary to hand out or sell 88s to various nations that were either allied to or sympathetic to Germany's war aims, despite the ever-increasing need to equip the German armed forces with as many anti-aircraft guns as could be manufactured.

One of the very first transfers of 88s came with the sale of a batch of about eighteen 8.8cm FlaK 18s to Argentina. This was a commercial sale negotiated directly with Krupp AG, which delivered the guns to Buenos Aires in about 1938. Once in Argentina, the guns defended the national capital for many years up to and after 1945 but apparently never fired a shot in anger.

Another pre-1939 transfer involved the guns taken to Spain by the German Condor Legion of 'volunteers' fighting alongside the Nationalists during the civil war. They initially took with them four four-gun batteries of 8.8cm FlaK 18s and a fifth battery arrived soon after to form what became known as the *FlaK Abteilung 88*, or F/88. Contrary to general belief these German-held guns were retained primarily for the air-defence role and rarely fired at ground targets.

More 88s arrived for issue direct to the Spanish Nationalists as the war progressed. It was the Nationalists, always short of up-to-date artillery, who pioneered the use of the 88 against ground targets – German observers duly made note of the fact and reported back to Berlin accordingly. When the Germans left Spain in 1939 they left all their guns in Spain to be adopted as one of the mainstays of Spain's air defences. By 1945 their numbers, including 88 examples of the FlaK 36, had grown to 140. More were to be added later (see below).

Once Italy entered the war alongside Germany in 1941 it was found necessary to pass large amounts of German war materiel to their new combat ally since the equipment levels of the Italian armed forces were dangerously low and often of poor quality. This particularly applied to anti-aircraft guns for although the Italians already had a gun as good as the German 88 in production, they did not have enough of them and their ability to manufacture more was limited. The Italian gun was the Ansaldo *Cannone da 90/53 CA*, which was ordered into series production in 1939 but by mid-1943 only 539 had been delivered in static, towed,

The 8.8cm FlaK 18s on parade in this photograph are believed to be part of the batch sold to Argentina in 1938. The tractors are either Pavesi or Fiat/Spa models. (P Chamberlain Collection)

An 8.8cm FlaK 18 in action in North Africa with Italian troops. The Italians knew the 88 as the Cannone da 88/56 CA modello 18-36. (P Chamberlain Collection)

armoured vehicle and truck-borne forms. Once in service the guns were added to the array of somewhat ancient and varied guns already in the Italian anti-aircraft gun inventory and some were diverted to coast-defence duties. While numbers of *Cannone da 90/53 CA* did see field service in North Africa, the Germans saw fit to eke out their numbers by handing over a number of 88s to the Italians, who took them over as the *Cannone da 88/56 CA modello 18-36*. The exact number is not known but all remaining examples still in Italy reverted to German ownership after the Italian armistice of July 1943.

Once the German take-over of Czecho-Slovakia was completed during 1939 the new state of Slovakia came into being already aligned with Germany. The new state assumed their share of the old Czecho-Slovak military inventory, the heavy anti-aircraft gun park being largely made up of *Škoda 8.35 cm kanon PL vzor 22/24* pieces from a previous design generation. As the Slovak Army was assigned to duties in support of Operation Barbarossa, the Germans decided to hand over 24 8.8cm FlaK 36 and 37 guns (along with a wide array of other military equipment), the first 4 of them arriving during March 1941, together with the first batches of what would become a total of 17,280 rounds of ammunition. By March 1944 the outstanding twenty guns, all of them /2 carriage static guns, had been added to the original four. Most of these guns were retained for home defence, and served on with the restored Czecho-Slovakian state after 1945.

Finland had a somewhat confusing war posture between 1939 and 1945, at times being allied with Germany and at other times being hostile. In 1941 Finland was on the side of Germany because of their desire to redress their defeat and loss of territory following the 1939–1940 Winter War with the Soviet Union. Germany's 1941 invasion of the Soviet Union gave Finland the opportunity to participate in what they termed their Continuation War. Over the years the Finnish air-defence arm had managed to accumulate a motley collection of anti-aircraft guns from all over Europe. During 1943 these were supplemented when the Finnish state purchased 18 towed 8.8cm FlaK 37 guns from Germany to equip 3 6-gun, anti-aircraft batteries defending Helsinki. These three batteries were controlled by three imported *Kommandogerät 40* fire-control predictors, known locally as the *Lambda*.

A further seventy-two FlaK 37s were acquired during 1944, this time on /2 static mountings. Of these, 36 guns were assigned to the defence of Helsinki, with Kotka, Tampere and Turku each receiving 2 6-gun batteries. There was also a twelve-gun battery at Kaivopuisto, another part of the defences of Helsinki. All these guns served on until well after 1945. The Finns knew their guns as the *88mm: n ilmatorjuntakanuuna vuodelta 1937 mallia Rheinmetall-Borsig* (ItK/37 RMB), for some reason allocating their provenance to Rheinmetall-Borsig (although reference has been found to an alternative RT).

Perhaps the most unusual end-users of the 88 during the war years were the Allies. By late 1944 the Allied land forces in Europe had advanced so far from their cross-Channel supply resources that front-line supply stocks often ran dangerously low during bad weather or when shortages of transport arose. Those supplies included artillery ammunition so it became a common expedient

American gunners emplacing a suitably marked captured 8.8cm PaK 43 for use against its former owners. (US National Archives)

for front-line units to turn the considerable quantities of captured artillery equipments against their former owners and use up any available stocks of captured ammunition.

Both British and American batteries employed such measures, the US Army going as far as forming 'Z Batteries', specifically to utilise captured artillery and ammunition, within their field artillery battalions. At one stage, in November 1944, the US First Army's 32nd Field Artillery Brigade created two provisional battalions that were fully equipped with captured German artillery equipments. Included in the captured haul were 8.8cm FlaK and PaK guns, 10.5cm and 15cm field howitzers and French 155mm GPF guns previously adopted by the Germans. This impressment of captured 88s by the Allies was a battlefield expedient that usually lasted only as long as the captured ammunition stocks lasted. However, as early as June 1943 the US Army did go to the extent of preparing and issuing a service manual for the 8.8cm FlaK 36 (TM E9-369A) following extensive technical studies carried out on equipments captured in Tunisia.

Post 1945

Once the Second World War was over most German 88s were either scrapped or relegated to being war trophies or museum pieces. Yet some European nations, having inherited heaps of weapons once the German armed forces had left the countries they had formerly occupied, decided to arm their newly emergent armed forces with German weapons, at least until something better could be obtained (usually via American military aid). These weapons included the 8.8cm FlaK 18/36/37 series – no PaK 43 series weapons seem to have been adopted by any nation after 1945, although many of their technical innovations were studied and often utilised.

Numerous nations fell into this category. This included Norway, which took over no less than 360 88s out of a total of 505 left behind when the Germans departed, the balance being mostly scrapped before the Allies decided that they might be useful to defend post-war Norway. The *Luftwaffe* had organised these guns into four FlaK Brigades headquartered at Oslo (173 guns), Stavanger (86 guns), Vaernes (86 guns) and Tromsø (158 guns). Some of the guns involved had a dual air-defence/coast-defence role and where possible the Norwegians simply took over the existing installations.

The Norwegian total of 360 guns included 141 towed FlaK 36, plus 15 in static installations. There were also 55 towed FlaK 37s and 139 static. These guns served on until the early 1950s when they began to be supplemented and then replaced in the air-defence role by numbers of American 90mm Gun M1A1 and M2s. Even then the 88s soldiered on because in 1957 125 88mm guns were transferred to the coast artillery. In this role they lasted only until the mid-1960s when they were withdrawn as part of a policy to limit Norwegian coast-artillery equipments to those with calibres of 105mm, 127mm and 150mm (all former German naval guns) to ease the training and logistic situation. Norway investigated the adoption of the 8.8cm PaK 43/41 (possibly for employment as a coast-defence gun) but it does not appear to have been accepted for their service.

Other post-war user nations included Yugoslavia, where some guns were assigned to coast defence installed in specially constructed concrete bunkers having overhead protection. Another post-1945 user was Czecho-Slovakia, which took in any remaining FlaK 41s in addition to the other FlaK models; all were eventually replaced by Soviet equipments. A few Yugoslav 88s reportedly survived to see limited action during the Balkan Troubles of the 1990s.

France also adopted 88s abandoned once the Germans had left France, sending numbers of FlaK guns to be used in their post-war Indo-China campaigns along with an array of ex-Second World War (and even First World War) artillery relics, including former Japanese artillery pieces. The French 88s had nothing to do with air defence once they got to Indo-China as the local opposition did not have any aircraft assets, so the guns were employed in the direct- or indirect-fire artillery role. As such they were probably the last 88s to take part in a full-scale, live shooting war.

Other nations adopted the 88 as a long-term measure, one of them being Finland. By 1945 that nation had accumulated numerous types of anti-aircraft gun but they regarded the ninety FlaK 37s they had acquired during 1943 and 1944 as the best in their inventory. The guns emplaced around various Finnish cities were retained until 1969 as air-defence weapons (the last personnel assigned to them were trained during 1967) and even then their service careers continued. The guns were passed to the Coast Artillery arm where they soldiered on until the end of the twentieth century. At first they were installed as mobile, low-trajectory coast-defence weapons but gradually they were relegated to training duties and eventually to simply firing during exercises to conserve ammunition that would otherwise have been fired by more modern weapons, a role an ever-decreasing number of 88s is still performing to this day. Many guns are still held in storage as reserve weapons, although their possible utility as such seems more unlikely as the years progress. Ammunition for these guns was manufactured locally by the concern that, after several name changes, became Patria Vammas.

Perhaps the most involved user nation of the 88 after 1945 was Spain. By 1945 the numbers of FlaK 18 and 36 guns sent to Spain, in attempts to keep Spain's General Franco at least sympathetic to the Germany cause, had reached 140. An

Looking rather forlorn and neglected, this Finnish 8.8cm FlaK 37 (ItK/37 RMB) was still being used for training firings as late as 2007. (TJ Gander)

additional ploy to keep Spain on the German side was to offer manufacturing licences for various German weapon designs, among them being the 8.8cm FlaK 18. Licence negotiations commenced as early as May 1941 but it took time to establish the required manufacturing facilities, not the least difficulty being obtaining the necessary raw materials and machine tools at a time when Europe was at war.

An initial order for fifty-six guns was issued during 1941 but progress was at first slow. Orders for components and sub-assemblies were distributed to numerous contractors around Spain, the final assembly centre and prime contractor being the Fábrica de Trubia at Oviedo, from which came the designation of the Spanish 88s, namely FT-44, or *Fábrica de Trubia Mod 1944* (the full designation was *Cañón Antiaéreo de 88/56 milímetros modelo FT-44*).

The FT-44 emerged as a hybrid model comprising the one-piece FlaK 18 pattern barrel, the *Sonderanhänger 202* of the FlaK 36 and the fire-control data-transmission system of the FlaK 37. The first FT-44 appeared during June 1943 but it was not until 1946 that any degree of series production commenced and then only at a leisurely rate of about twelve a year. The production rate increased to twenty-four a year between 1948 and 1950 before settling back to twelve a year until 1955. Production then ceased for a while before a few more were completed

Typical of many 88 gate guardians to be seen today, this ex-Spanish FT-44 can be seen at the Occupation Museum at Forest on Guernsey. (TJ Gander)

by 1962, the final plan being to produce 250 complete equipments. This final total appears never to have been reached, a total of 226 being the more likely. In 1958 there were 204 FT-44s in service with the Spanish Army and land units of the Spanish Navy.

One attempt was made to boost the all-round performance of the FT-44 by the development of a 72-calibre barrel placed on a suitably modified FT-44 mounting. The *Pieza de 88/72* remained a prototype.

Another attempt to boost the FT-44's performance came with the development of a 70mm sub-calibre projectile developed by the *Centro de Estudios Técnocos de Materiales Especiales* (CETME). When fired this saboted sub-calibre projectile had a muzzle velocity of 1,050m/s, resulting in a maximum ceiling of 13,500m compared to the 10,600m of a conventional projectile. The sub-projectile weighed 5.4kg on firing, reducing to 4.6kg after the sabots had fallen away. The high-explosive payload weighed 490g.

Another project that did not leave the prototype hardware stage was the *Pieza de 88/56 mm 'Galileo'*, an attempt to adapt the power-laying system of the Bofors 40/70 anti-aircraft gun to allow the rapid on-carriage laying of the FT-44. The fire-control system, based on an Italian Officine Galileo design, enabled a single

Details of the Guernsey FT-44. The breech block is missing. (TJ Gander)

layer to aim and fire the gun using a joystick control arrangement that actuated electro-hydraulic powered controls to achieve rapid barrel movements in both elevation and traverse. With the prototype, aiming relied on a simple cartwheel sight, although the barrel could be pointed towards a potential target by a No. 3 Mark 7 search radar. No doubt some form of reflex sight coupled to a computerised predictor unit would have eventually replaced the 'iron' cartwheel sight. While such a control system may have had numerous advantages for a more responsive automatic gun such as the Bofors 40/70, its employment on a non-automatic gun such as the FT-44 was more questionable. A single prototype was converted to the Galileo configuration but it did not progress very far.

By the late 1960s the air-defence value of the FT-44 against modern high-speed aircraft was becoming debatable so they were gradually withdrawn and placed in reserve storage. Beginning in 1972, some conversions were made to allow FT-44 carriages to be utilised as missile launchers for a coast-defence guided missile based on a scaled-down Hawk air-defence missile, the main modification being the replacement of the barrel and its associated sub-components by two short lengths of missile launcher rail to launch two missiles. Although hardware examples of the missile system were produced, the project was terminated.

By the early 1990s the remaining FT-44s were gradually being sold off to film companies and military equipment enthusiasts, many ending up as gate guardians at locations all around the world. Many of the 88s to be seen today will be revealed as Spanish FT-44s.

Chapter 6

Making a Legend

Any account relating to the German 88s must make mention of why, even now, the gun is still regarded in what are almost legendary terms. Numerous accolades continue to be showered upon the reputation of the 88, usually along the lines of 'The Most Famous Gun of the Second World War', 'Germany's Secret Weapon' and so on, but it is hoped that the descriptions and accounts given in these pages will have revealed that the 88 was, in gun design and ballistic terms, nothing very special for its time.

This somewhat bland statement does not intend to denigrate the fearful effect the 88 had on many battles between 1940 and 1945. As has been described, in its heyday the armour-penetration capabilities of the 88 were prodigious, while its effect on Allied bomber crews was such that it grew to be understandably respected by them as well. Yet the simple fact remains that the 88 was only one anti-aircraft gun among many others of the same design generation. Other contemporary anti-aircraft guns could match or excel its all-round performance relating in terms of muzzle velocity, projectile weight, operational ceilings and so forth. Where they could not match the 88 was in its tactical handling and mobility, topics that will be dealt with below.

To give a quick impression of the ballistic performances of the 88 and just a couple of its contemporaries, a simple check-list should suffice:

Gun	MV (HE)	Ceiling	Proj Wt (HE)	Wt in action
8.8cm FlaK 36	820m/s	8,000m	9kg	7,200kg
Brit 3.7in	792m/s	9,800m	12.7kg	9,300kg
US 90mm Gun M1A1	823m/s	9,800m	10.43kg	8,600kg

From these rounded-off figures it can be seen that in many respects the British 3.7in (94mm) Anti-Aircraft Gun and the American 90mm Gun M1A1 could outperform the German 88 in almost every detail. Yet the 3.7in gun was an almost direct contemporary of the 88 in development terms and the 90mm Gun M1A1 dated from only a few years after. Where the Allied guns could not score was in combat weight, for both of the Allied guns were much bulkier and heavier than their German counterpart, making them that much more difficult to move.

One of the reasons for the 88's continuing fame is connected with approach rather than anything else. To the Allies an anti-aircraft gun was an anti-aircraft gun and nothing else. Both the Allied guns mentioned above had been designed to shoot at aircraft and with nothing else in mind. The entire design approach had therefore been to make the guns as effective in that role as could be achieved. That entailed all manner of technical accessories, such as powered carriage drives, powered rammers, fuse-setting machines, stable firing platforms and even ammunition-handling devices. The end result was that both the Allied guns mentioned above emerged as suitable for little other than their intended role, that of anti-aircraft guns.

Not surprisingly this dedicated-role approach extended to the Allied gunners who had to utilise the guns in action. They employed their guns for what they

Looking rather crowded, a fully crewed 8.8cm FlaK 18. (P Chamberlain Collection)

An 8.8cm FlaK 18 with its long 56-calibre barrel strewn with wired-on branches to break up the outline of the barrel. (TJ Gander Collection)

were designed for, namely shooting at aircraft. They were not equipped, trained or inclined to use their cherished guns for any other purpose. Consequently, both the British and US Armies retained their anti-aircraft guns to defend their rear areas and important-point targets likely to attract the attention of enemy aircraft. The mere thought of towing their bulky guns into forward areas to engage land targets was quite simply not an option. Dragging towed loads the size of a 3.7in gun or 90mm M1 across open battlefields within visual and artillery range of the enemy was something most gunners would not care to think about. Only rarely were Allied anti-aircraft guns employed in a ground-to-ground firing role and that was mainly confined to adding their fire to the 'pepper pot' indirect artillery barrages conducted during the latter stages of the 1944–1945 land campaigns in north-east Europe when no airborne targets were likely to appear. One notable exception occurred as early as May 1940 when a single 3.7in anti-aircraft battery destroyed four German tanks approaching the Channel port of Boulogne. This isolated incident seems to have gone unnoticed at the time, no doubt due to other more pressing events in progress and the fact that the battery itself became a casualty of the action.

It should not be overlooked that the Germans started the Second World War with the same set of conceptions as the Allies. While their participation in the Spanish Civil War may have provided them with many insights into the nature of modern warfare, the deployment of their FlaK guns in Spain remained firmly in

Luftwaffe hands and, being air-minded, their prime remit was to provide air defence. They did observe the Spanish Nationalist forces employing their 88s (and many other types of artillery weapon) in the direct-fire role against armoured vehicles and field fortifications but only rarely did the German 'volunteers' indulge in such practices, and then only in emergencies – they belonged to an air arm, not land combat forces. But they did report their direct-firing observations back to Berlin, where the reports were duly noted. A few adventurous staff officers then decided to take matters further and carry out numerous field trials of their own, usually with the fortified defences of the French Maginot Line in mind.

It was at this point that the German and Allied philosophies diverged. The German approach to war was entirely pragmatic and flexible. When British and French tanks were encountered during the Battle for France in mid-1940 the German method of engaging the enemy armour was to utilise whatever was to hand, from mortars to field artillery pieces, together with light and heavy FlaK guns, including the 88. The effectiveness of the 88 against heavily armoured British and French tanks was soon appreciated and from then onwards the 88 was regarded as a dual-purpose weapon. But this role change could not have been successfully achieved without the seemingly inherent tactical flexibility of German soldiers and their ready acceptance of new challenges and change. Despite the numerous tales of iron discipline and strict adherence to orders relating to the German soldier, usually promulgated by Allied propaganda, the truth was often very different. German combat personnel, including those of the *Luftwaffe*, were encouraged to use their personal initiative and improvisation to the full in whatever tactical circumstances they found themselves. Thus if an improvised combat ploy or unusual approach to a tactical situation was demonstrated to be effective, it was often adopted, broadcast and employed until its utility either vanished or could be improved upon.

Thus it was with the hasty deployment of a line of 88s during the Arras fighting in 1940, a deployment that ultimately formalised and drove home the effectiveness of the 88 against tanks. From then onwards the 88 was frequently used in the anti-armour role, despite the shortcomings of the gun for the task. As described elsewhere, the 88 was too high, bulky, heavy and difficult to hide, all important drawbacks for the anti-tank role, but that did not bother the Germans. They simply adopted the fact that firing their 88s against tanks was effective, even at long ranges. Recognising that their other specialised anti-tank guns had become inadequate, details such as weapon handling, concealment and tactical deployment relating to the 88 were worked out and converted into standard operational techniques. Only rarely did the Allies display a similar flexibility of approach towards similar tactical challenges, hence their adherence to utilising their anti-aircraft guns simply as anti-aircraft guns – and nothing else.

At one stage during 1941 the British in North Africa did indeed follow a path similar to the German adoption of the anti-armour 88 but it was with their 25-pounder gun-howitzers. These field pieces were pressed into the anti-tank role in North Africa for the same reason that the Germans turned to their 88. The standard British anti-tank gun, the 2-pounder with a calibre of 40mm, had demonstrated that it was virtually useless against the latest generation of tanks. As there was apparently nothing else to hand, according to the contemporary way of thinking, the 25-pounder had to assume a role for which it had never been intended. The 3.7in anti-aircraft guns guarding the Suez Canal and other rear areas were not even considered as potential anti-tank weapons.

While the 25-pounder may have had a calibre almost identical to that of the German 88 (namely 87.6mm), being a gun-howitzer it had a much lower maximum muzzle velocity (only 518m/s) and had to rely on firing high-explosive projectiles only until a solid-shot, armour-piercing equivalent could be hurriedly developed and issued.

There was also the problem of range. Tank targets had to approach to ranges of less than 900m for the British (and Commonwealth) gunners to be sure of a hit and significant resultant damage. Gunners therefore had to stand their ground until their targets came into effective range which, in the open deserts of North Africa, exposed them to hostile long-range tank-gun and machine-gun fire, usually resulting in guns and their crews being knocked out of action before they could usefully open fire. In addition the 25-pounder's times in and out of action were dangerously long and not helped by the prime mover, the lightly armoured Quad tractor, being notoriously prone to catching fire when hit. During 1941 casualties among guns and gunners were horrendous but the crews persisted in their anti-armour role for if a 25-pounder (11.34kg) high-explosive projectile did strike a tank the results could be devastating. One saving grace for the 25-pounders was the circular firing platform that formed one of the main design features of the piece. Once the carriage wheels were on the platform one member of the gun crew could lift the trail and introduce rapid traverse movements of up to 360° with ease, enabling the barrels to be pointed towards new targets within seconds. The ordeals of the 25-pounder crews lasted into 1942 before the replacement for the 2-pounder, namely the 6-pounder anti-tank gun, arrived in sufficient numbers to allow the 25-pounders to reassume their primary role.

Comparisons between the 88 and the 25-pounder may be invidious as they were very different artillery weapons, yet they pressed home the reasons why the German 88 proved to be such a relative success, while the 25-pounder anti-tank era proved to be an expensive improvisation that many gunners of the time did not wish to experience again.

There was another reason for the fame of the 88 and it arose from an incorrect initial premise. All the early participants in what became the Second World War commenced operations with some accepted ideas regarding armoured warfare that turned out to be erroneous, most of them relating to vehicle armour, its penetration and their main armament. In 1939 tanks on all sides were still relatively lightly armoured (apart from a few specialised infantry support vehicles) and their gun calibres were too small. Generally speaking, all sides developed tank armour and anti-tank guns that could be effective only against what they themselves possessed. If a nation's tank was proof against the

Typical of the design imbalance of many tanks of the early war years was the Matilda II. Although it was very well armoured and proof against most contemporary anti-tank guns, it was under gunned with a 2-pounder gun and very slow and ponderous. (P Chamberlain Collection)

fire of the nation's standard anti-tank gun that was deemed acceptable and the tank itself did not need to arm itself with anything heavier in the main armament line. Combat experience was to demonstrate the hazards of this approach, the ultimate recognition only occurring when German anti-tank gunners watched their carefully aimed projectiles bouncing off British and French tank armour in 1940. The most numerous German tank gun of that period was still the same ineffectual 37mm gun as used by the German anti-tank gunners. (In 1940 nearly all American tanks carried a similar 37mm main gun.)

That the 88 was to have such a dramatic influence on the tussle between tank armour and anti-tank guns should therefore now come as not too much of a surprise. The firepower, projectile weight and combat range of the 88 made a tremendous impact on all who had to undergo the experience, but that experience was on such a lethal scale that terms of 'secret weapon' or 'wonder weapon' began to be bandied about, not only in soldiers' conversations but in media accounts that attempted to disguise the reasons why the 88 was having such an impression. The fact was that the British, French and, to a marginally lesser extent, the Germans had badly underestimated the basic requirements of armoured combat-vehicle design.

Regarded by many as the best of all the anti-tank guns fielded during the Second World War, the 8.8cm PaK 43 was also the most powerful of all the German 88s. (US National Archives)

Any successful combat vehicle still has to display three basic and balanced design factors, namely firepower, protection and mobility. Ignoring or neglecting any one (or more) of these factors results in an unsatisfactory solution to providing a viable combat vehicle. For instance, the British focused heavily on mobility and tended to neglect firepower and (in most cases) protection, relying on mobility alone for a degree of protection, such as with their Cruiser tank series. When they did emphasise protection, as with their infantry support tanks, firepower was neglected, while the same vehicles proceeded only at the speed of a marching soldier.

Even if they were way ahead in tank tactics, the Germans were little better off in tank-design terms in 1939, but they did manage to stay just one step ahead in almost every aspect of tank technology until 1945. Compared to their Allied counterparts, German tanks were seemingly always better armed, better protected and more mobile throughout the war years, the heavy Tiger I and Tiger II being notable exceptions as they lacked mobility. The Allies lauding the 88 as a 'wonder weapon' helped in some degree to disguise that fact. In the process they completely overlooked the corresponding reality that British and American tank designers were just as inherently capable of turning out similar combat vehicles and guns had they utilised a concentrated, ruthlessly determined approach similar to that of their German counterparts, an approach that free-thinking civilians in uniform could never adopt.

When the war ended in 1945 the 88 was still a potent weapon, while the arrival of the specialised tank and anti-tank 88s only served to prolong the 'wonder weapon' identity. So good was their all-round performance that 88s served on for years with many nations after 1945 – but so did the British 3.7in Anti-Aircraft Gun and the American 90mm Gun M1A1.

Bibliography

The following sources are those that are generally accessible. Many of the details contained in these pages have been culled from numerous other sources such as copies of intelligence reports, odd articles and personal contacts.

Canadian Military Headquarters. *Artillery Equipments*, Vol 3, London, 1945

Chamberlain, P and Gander, T. *88 FlaK and PaK*, Windsor, Profile Publications Ltd, 1976

Chamberlain, P and Gander, T. *Small Arms, Artillery and Special Weapons of the Third Reich*, London, Macdonald and Jane's, 1978

Delsert, B, Dubois, J and Kowal, C. *La FlaK 1914–1918*, two vols, Lagniieu, La Plume du Temps, 2000

Farndale, Gen Sir M. *History of the Royal Regiment of Artillery, The Years of Defeat 1939–41*, London, Brasseys, 1996

Gander, T. *Germany's Guns 1939–45*, Ramsbury, Crowood Press, 1998

Garcia, J, Franco, L and Perez, A. 'La Maquinaa y la Historia No. 16', *Historia de la Artilleria Antiaerea Espanola*, Vol 1, Valladolid, Quiron Ediciones, 1998

Hahn, F. *Waffen und Geheimwaffen des deutschen Heeres 1933–1945*, Koblenz, Bernard & Graefe Verlag, 1986

Illustrated Record of German Artillery Equipment 1939–1945, Vol II, Part II, London, 1948

Liddel Hart, B. *The Rommel Papers*, London, Collins, 1953

Hogg, I. *German Artillery of World War Two*, London, Arms and Armour Press, 1975

Horne, A. *To Lose a Battle France 1940*, London, PAPERMAC, 1990

Müller, W. *The Heavy FlaK Guns*, West Chester, PA, Schiffer Publishing Ltd, 1990

Perez, A. *La Fabrica De Trubia*, Gijon, Fvndacion Alvargonzalez, n.d.

TM E-9 369A German 88-mm Antiaircraft Gun Materiel, Washington, 1943

Vehvviläinen, R, Lappi, A and Palokangas, M. *Itsenäisen Suomen Ilmatorjuntatykit 1917–2000*, Helsinki, Sotamuseo, 2005

Index